You Can Always Get What You Want

Your Starter Package for Personal Success

by

Phil Murray

First published by PeRFECT WORDS and MUSIC in 1993

Copyright © 1993 Phil Murray

British Library Cataloguing-in-Publication Data available

ISBN 1-898716-00-5

Printed in Great Britain by
Lambda Business Services

Birches Industrial Estate, Imberhorne Lane,
East Grinstead, Sussex RH19 1XZ, ENGLAND.
Telephone 0342 312167

Dedicated to Ali, Luke and Eve...

with all my Love

Foreward

The writing and researching of this book has been the most exciting experience of my life. My discoveries have made a personal dream come true, and being able to share them with you is a bonus.

I always knew that there was more to life than was immediately apparent. I felt that if I looked hard enough, in all the right places, the big secret would jump out at me.

It did.

The big secret was no secret at all. Nobody had been hiding it from me . . . I had been concealing it from myself.

Way back in 1976, I had begun to set myself goals and targets, with fine reasons for being, and purposes galore! I had plans. I studied hard, and worked late. I was nearly successful, then I wasn't . . . by 1984 I had embarked upon a path for financial success, and departed my spiritual studies forever . . . or so I thought.

It wasn't until the 2nd of January, 1993, that I had the cognition that really lit the fuse and got the rocket moving. The bonus, was in the realisation that my spiritual ideals were in no way compromised by my new strategy for success. In fact the exact reverse was true. I had more spiritual gain in my quest for riches, than I ever had whilst seeking the truth.

In this book, I have outlined a route to success.

You can travel this route if you want, or you can seek out your own path. Either way, if you are successful, then we will be utilising the same technology.

This is a starter package.

I believe that you can be successful by utilising the technology contained in this volume alone, and marrying it to whatever is already within you; but I know that you will miss out on the slants and nuances of a thousand minds if you do not take your studies further.

The bibliography at the end of the book is for this purpose. There, you will find many of the works that I myself have studied...but I have excluded some. If I gained from a book, or a piece of data, that I did not believe was completely wholesome, then I have not mentioned it.

Don't fight it...drop your defences...lower your guard...and follow me on a mind expanding experience. Accompany me on a wealth increasing mission, and set *no limits* to what you can achieve.

You can do it. I know you can, and what's more important...YOU know you can.

Have a good trip!

Phil Murray

Contents

You Can Always Get What You Want

Your Starter Package for Personal Success

stage one

are you ready for this?

Begin with the end in mind . . .   *Stephen R Covey*

This question of readiness you must answer honestly if you are to get maximum benefits from your new life!

I want you to buy this book, and the chances are that you are browsing through the pages in some bookstore, looking for a good reason why you should part company with your hard earned cash, and if I don't hit you hard in the first few paragraphs, your money could go on something else.

Okay . . . here goes . . .

I know the Secret of Success and you don't!

That is why you need this book. I can honestly say that if you are ready for lasting success, this book will give you the missing ingredients. I discovered this secret from someone else, who in turn discovered it personally from some of the most famous and successful people this world has ever known.

I hope that is a good enough reason to go and pay for the book. It is . . . good!

To the business in hand. I want to present you with facts, as well as inspirational ideas. I have a duty to motivate you . . . but I am just the starter motor . . . *the size of your personal success will depend entirely on your dedication to being successful.* You can't get success just through buying a book. You have to want it badly, and *do* something about it. You have to see it as the best option, and you have to pay the price that success will demand of you.

Lots of people know the secret of success, and can tell you it. The secret contained within the secret, is that the greatest of the ingredients lies within you, and the success itself will not be forthcoming until you act upon the various elements of the equation without compromise.

I have been in the entertainment business all of my life. This does not lessen the validity of this material, nor does it mean that I am playing for the laughs or trying for the tears as I sing the song. I believe that I have approached the field of human behavioural improvement from a sensible base, and have housed it in a very strong structure.

When I worked one night stands, which is a baptism of fire for life itself, I was of the opinion that I should charge as much as the market would stand for my performance. I always said that if I had to make the effort to perform, it would be the same effort for a low fee as it would be for a high fee. I would perform for the same length of time. I always asked for the high fee and I usually got it!

It's the same in life. You are going to be playing the game whether you like it or not. The same time is needed for a life of poor quality as is needed for a life of success. This is not totally true as there is room to argue that you will allow yourself a longer life if it is to be pleasurable, but this part of the book is not the right place for that argument. What I am saying, is that you may as well concentrate on success. You may as well focus on the positive side of your personality.

I had a partner for a time, who felt that if we charged less for our performance, we would get more work. I said that I didn't want to play the venues that couldn't pay the money, and suggested that we increase our fee, as other artistes were decreasing theirs because of the recession. I wanted to position ourselves in the marketplace at a certain level.

Life is a marketplace and you have to position yourself in it. Are you a club singer, or cabaret? Do you write your own material, or use other peoples'? Do you give good value for money, or do you try to sneak off early? Are you chart material, or still waiting to get into the business? Do you record albums that will last, or singles for the moment?

Will your new album still be played in sixty years time?

The same act could be seen in entirely different situations, and where the act was seen bore as much responsibility for someone's opinion of that act, as the quality of the act itself.

If I told you that I had written songs for The Beatles, or some other successful unit, you would give me a listen. If I said that "I was doing the clubs", and still had a day job, I'd have more trouble. I *always*

13

believe that the world is waiting for a Phil Murray song.

Is the world waiting for you?

Other people have positioned you in the market-place. Where have you placed yourself? If you positioned yourself higher, is that how you would be seen?

People usually reach their target. Did you know that? What you are aiming for you will usually get? You have to ask yourself if you are *going for gold*!

I had a guitarist who insisted that he was happy as long as he had his beer and cigarettes. Some of the band felt that he had a good attitude and was easily pleased. He was! I was relieved when he left the band because I felt that his expectations were too low... but I noticed that he never went without his beer and cigarettes... and those two things were all he ever got out of the band that we were once both in together.

The more that you demand from your life, the more you will get out of it.

Simple isn't it?

If you are tired of the same old you, and think that there is nothing new and exciting lurking just around that corner...then you are in for a surprise.

Are you tired of what you are, and think that there is no way of improvement...if the answer to that

14

question is yes, then change your mind and *brace yourself for lift off*!

I'm telling you right now that if you expect more from your life than you ever previously thought possible, you will get it.

Demand improvement!

You have bought this book so you must be after something more from your life. What I ask of you, is that as well as psyching yourself up with the positive affirmations contained in this material...as well as allowing me to psyche you up with a short term fix of well being...as well as jumping up and down shouting yeah, yeah, yeah with your pants around your ankles, and then rejoicing in the new experience of knowing that you can do anything that you want... *spare a thought for the future*. Make a long term commitment to yourself for now, and forever.

Commit yourself to a policy of continuous improvement for every aspect of your life!

Make that deal with yourself, and as general as it is, your life can only get better. As your life improves in it's various ways, then your Family and friends will not only notice a positive change in you, but they will also experience a change in their own fortunes, which will then lead them on in turn to make efforts for their own self improvement, which will of course reflect positively on you. So you see how easy it is for you to create a positive momentum . . . with you at the helm.

Endorse that policy now.

Continuous improvement for every aspect of your life!

With every self improvement programme, you have to watch out for the Chinese meal syndrome. Great while you are eating it, and for an hour or so afterwards, but it isn't long before you are empty again.

This one book is not going to be the end of your bid for a better life. It's a taster . . . a tempting morsel . . . an indication of what is on offer out there. You have to scout around and find out ways of bettering yourself that are relevant to you and your life style. Different authors have styles that suit people in various ways.

I am for the *Positive Attitude* movement. I believe that a positive attitude can surmount the insurmountable. I *believe that you can move mountains*. I believe that even the most miserable, snivelling, grovelling, creeping, failure of an excuse for a human being, can be shown the way to success both as a person, and in life itself. Still, I do hope that not too many of you reading this right now fit that particular description, and if you do . . . good on you for recognising that a change is needed.

My style is to go for the jugular . . . a kind of "it's there so do it" attitude. You will find gentler approaches . . . a velvet glove instead of my boxing

16

glove. What I am saying is, the technology for self improvement is there and available, without a shadow of a doubt. Your own success is there for the taking. Don't be put off by the carrier wave or the messenger. It's you that has to improve and change for the better. . . not me that has to improve you. I will help, but the ultimate responsibility is yours.

I always wonder at people trying to give up habits they no longer require. Smoking is the obvious example, but the theory applies to any change you may wish to bring about. A friend of mine told me that he'd just sampled the new nicotine patches that have just become widely available, and they had worked as well as the hypnotist and the chewing gum that he'd tried previously. . . in other words not at all! I told him that they worked well enough, but it was him that wasn't working properly, expecting something else to do the job for him. He expected magic, and didn't like the non sympathetic approach that I offered him, but he did take note.

I am not saying that I believe in the General Patton approach every time; but you must know that a world of difference exists between an aid, or something that helps you, and the actual decision by you to accomplish something. You can't ever blame an aid, and also claim to be wholly responsible for yourself. You can search for better help. That is taking responsibility. You have to know that you, are at the end of every line. When all the excuses are made, if the job has not been done, if the bed has not been made, the sale has not been closed, or the change

17

has not been made for the better...you are still there.

Enjoy responsibility.

This subject of responsibility is just too large to be glossed over. I am ultimately talking about the fact that you have to take responsibility for every single aspect of this Universe, and the sooner you understand this principle, the easier your transition towards success will be.

After you get yourself into shape, you get yourself and your partner on an even keel, and the kids feeling good about themselves, then your group of friends talking positively about each and every member of that group that you are all a part of...you move onto your town, then your country, then neighbouring territories, then you are in shape to look at the Planet Earth...the Universe...can you can get this big a picture of things? You will!

And why not try it? It sure as hell beats gossip!

Surely a challenge of such magnitude is worth some effort. Can you get the idea of total responsibility? Could you pick someone else's litter up? Could you serve someone without telling them? Is anything beneath you? Can you foresee a time when you will place £10,000 worth of used banknotes into an envelope and give it to Oxfam.

Aspire towards being able to give away millions of pounds to GOOD CAUSES.

I often wonder what would happen if the Planet was invaded. Would warring nations forget their differences? I know that they would. The differences between the West and the old Soviet Union paled into insignificance whilst the threat of Nazism hung in the air. As soon as the Nazis were licked, all the old reasons for hating each other once more came out of the closet. It didn't have to be that way.

The Cold War came about because of a dismal web of mistrust and mismanaged communications between two super powers. Misunderstandings and propaganda fed an already existing fear of the unknown. Everyone focused on the differences of policy, and their own fear of change. How history itself would have changed, if the good points of both cultures had been embraced, and each side had focused on how it could help the other.

You have to be willing to move out of the comfort zone.

You must respond to your circumstances with action, based on honourable theory. You cannot become successful by remaining in your already existing situation. This is your comfort zone, and it takes no effort to stay there. That is part of the recipe for stagnation. Stay as you are. Fear of the unknown. Better the devil you know. Best not try anything new.

Bull.

You didn't buy this book to stay in the comfort zone, so let's start adding the ingredients of success to your life, and then see the difference when ACTION *is married to the* PRINCIPLES!

Are you willing to do whatever is necessary, to be successful?

THE FIRST STEP

If you hate anyone or anything, the only person who is harmed by that hate is you. The biggest and most valuable present you can give to yourself right now, is the gift of forgiveness! To forgive every single person whom you believe has committed a disservice to you, would free up so much energy you would be amazed.

Begin by forgiving yourself!

Sounds crazy doesn't it?

Forgive yourself for all the wrongs you have ever done to yourself and others. Do that right now! Stop blame, and introduce forgiveness. Don't regret anything that has happened in the past. You are going to start afresh, and before you can do that, you have to forgive yourself.

Then forgive your parents.

You don't have to tell them. No one need know. It's not a patronising act! Just forgive them for whatever you think they did wrong. It is next to impossible to go through life without building up disagreements with the people you love the most. The very fact that you love them, means that you will be around them, or at least their viewpoints, more than people you like less. The chance of disagreement heightens as one grows older. You begin to exert more self determination. The transition between childhood and adolescence is fraught with difficulty. Parents are totally responsible for a child one minute, and apparently not needed the next. Parents had to learn too. Parents aren't fully qualified until they have experienced every aspect of parenthood, and that is usually when the job of "parenting" is complete and the necessary experience gained... too late!

Forgive your parents now and feel the relief immediately.

Continue this process, and rid yourself of all that negativity that you have been needlessly carrying around. I know... that thought of, "he doesn't deserve forgiveness", "why should I forgive her", "they did it to me first". Well, just forgive them for yourself.

Forgiveness is a selfish act.

Give yourself this present. Forgiveness is also a big move towards getting what you want from life, and your own personal success.

You will need all of the attention units that are

available to you for what lies ahead. You have to start creating habits that will benefit you. If you are ready for this personal success, then you have to able to prepare mentally for the future, and this takes brain power. Every single living person has the brain power that is necessary. Most people use this mental attention that is available to them, on irrelevancies. We allow junk mail and junk ideas to impinge on our thoughts. We allow junk newspapers to indoctrinate the population with junk gossip. We turn on the TV to watch another unstimulating junk programme. We eat junk food and wonder why the health of the body declines. We swallow junk propaganda and buy junk.

Do you see yourself as junk? No? Then don't tolerate junk.

Don't feed on junk.

The human mind is a great gift and needs to be used according to it's design. If you filled your petrol tank with diesel would it work properly? My job at this point in the book, is to get you into a receptive state of mind that will allow the technology of human improvement a chance. Some of you will have filled your heads so full of circuits and bad data up to this point in your lives . . . well I'm afraid you will just have to make an extra effort and push all that garbage to one side. We have to free up the brain, and put it to work *for us*, and not *against us*. ***Positive thinking is a habit that needs to be learned***.

I want you to join the PAC!

What's the PAC?

The Positive Attitudes Club.

As I am doing most of the work at the moment. . . I nominate myself Leader of the PAC. All you need to become a member, is commitment. You have to pledge allegiance to the idea that anything can be accomplished with a positive attitude. Until you do that you're a Learner. Once you have made a commitment to the PAC, then you become a Practitioner. With an accumulation of relevant knowledge, you will become an *Advanced* PAC *Practitioner*.

The aim of this book is to set you on course.

As a Practitioner, you make a further pledge to *change something for the better every day*. This begins within. You must continually eliminate the negative from your thought patterns. Don't worry, because you will be helped throughout this book. This help will only be apparent if you are a Practitioner. The Learners still haven't taken the plunge, and will need to pledge allegiance before the benefits of Club membership can be bestowed upon them.

As a PAC Member, you are entitled to a better life.

23

As you read this book, you will realise more and more that it essentially deals with the mental aspects of preparing you to achieve success, because the physical action necessary is entirely up to you. At no point has the fact escaped me that success can appear in many guises. I *also know that you all have different definitions of success*. You will soon realise that even if your sole purpose for reading this book is to get rich, then a by-product of that wealth will be spiritual gain. Transversely, if your main objective is spiritual gain, perhaps you will see the value of great wealth as we proceed.

If you decided that you would like to sail the Atlantic, you would need to train hard and organise yourself well. You would need to prepare your body for the constant motion. The boat would need attention. Your mind would have to be tuned in to the challenge. That is what I am doing with you right now. We are talking about forgiveness, and this is one thing that can give us a quick fix, a boost forward, a thrust from the engine . . . it can free up those attention units that we have decided as Practitioners we need, in order to proceed at full speed ahead.

I believe in this quick fix!

Forgiveness has been on the agenda forever. Just think of all the preachers and prophets who extolled the virtues of this simple little act throughout the ages. Do you think they talked about it for fun, or because it didn't work. It is a soul cleansing activity. A

24

hurdle to freedom. Jump it and see what is on the other side!

• • •

When was the last time you emptied your head? This can take a lot of practice, and I truly believe that some people go through life without ever being alone with themselves. Some call it meditation and some don't have a word for it because they can't conceive of the concept.

I just call it time to myself, or TTM, for short.

Great songs and ideas come to me during this TTM.

I can solve the problems of the world during this Time To Myself. It's a quality of life to me that I now could not be without. You have to make it happen. Those times when you say that you are too busy. . . they are just the times you need TTM.

Find a space where you can truly experience TTM. The top of a high mountain would be ideal, or the middle of the Pacific on a comfortable cruiser. Given that these ideals are unrealistic. . . try parking your car somewhere away from the sight of anyone else, in as quiet a place as possible. You may be fortunate enough to have a quiet room in your house. The location is for you to find. When you are practising TTM, you are not doing anything else. You are not thinking. That would be TFT, or Time For Thinking.

25

You are not listening, watching, eating, smoking, drinking or shuffling around in a chair.

Your ultimate goal is get out of yourself or exteriorise. We will talk later of the different parts of the Human Being. Knowing about this will be a major benefit, but it comes later. For now, we will aim for a peaceful environment without conscious thought. If solutions to problems appear for you, then fine. That is the Sub Conscious Mind working for you.

This TTM will eventually become the idea generator of your new life style, and will provide you with many answers to those problems that we both know are going to crop up from time to time. Treat TTM as essential, and not a luxury. You will discover a peaceful side to yourself amidst the hustle and bustle of the modern world.

When it is impractical to achieve true TTM, then you must create a space in your head to which you can retreat and recharge the batteries. I had a wonderful time down in the Florida Keys one year, and I have one particular picture to which I retreat when I feel a little overwhelmed.

I was with my wife and two children; we had just driven down from St Petersburg on our way to Key West, when we stopped on one of the first few Keys for a break. We believed that we had found Paradise. There was clean sand bordering the blue sea, hardly anyone around, and a stillness and serenity that you don't often find in holiday destinations. We looked out to a headland. The sun shone, and there was a lone palm tree gently swaying in the warm breeze.

26

I was brought up on the banks of the River Tyne in North East England. It is easy to see why such a picture had this kind of exhilarating effect on me.

The point is, that I use this picture and experience as a sanctuary. If I am worried about some kind of deadline, an upset in the Family or the cheque that hasn't arrived, I just "go to Florida". This isn't running away. It is an intelligent use of the facilities at my disposal.

A friend of ours used to tell us that not a day went by without her worrying about the World and it's problems. Boy, if you want to give yourself a sticky time, think about that imponderable. There is no point whatsoever in worrying about the World. This friend of ours could have come to Florida with us. In our Paradise, with a little TTM, we could have thought up one answer to one problem, acted on it, and done more for the world than the average town does in a year.

Great ideas people throughout the ages have used TTM to realise their place in history. Great inventions have been made with TTM, a pencil and some paper. People have earned their living by "sitting for ideas", using TTM. This literally meant that they would sit in quiet solitude, and allow their Sub Conscious Minds to present them with solutions to problems.

So, we have touched on some valuable points in this first stage of your journey on the way to personal success, and I think you are ready for the next. If you have joined the PAC and begun to take responsibility

27

for yourself and others; tackled the subject of forgiveness, and experienced TTM, then I think you are ready for

the secret of self esteem...

stage two

the secret of self esteem

>...the more you like yourself, the less you fear
>failure and rejection...   *Brian Tracy*

You have to like yourself before you can expect other people to like you.

I'm not talking about the big headed, empty vessel, vanity type of liking yourself. I'm talking about the real thing. A *genuine liking of the genuine article*.

For this liking to occur, you have to understand just how unique you are. There is no one walking this earth today who is the same as you. For this reason alone you are special. But if you add all the good ingredients that you know are there inside of you, to this original and unique Being who is you . . . do you begin to see that liking yourself is possible? Well I'm here to tell you that it is more than possible, it is pleasurable too.

My Father used to look in the mirror every day and say to whoever was within range, "How would you like to be as good looking as me?" He exuded confidence and of course I, like many boys with their Fathers, aspired to be just like him.

Occasionally we would have visitors, who would sometimes comment that my Father was big headed, but he wasn't. He just knew that he was good looking and didn't mind showing it. He could have been ugly but if he looked in the mirror every day and commented on his good looks, then you can bet your life he would have felt good looking, and that feeling would have transmitted itself to others and how they saw him.

That reminds me of the famous story about the early days of the motor car . . . and while we are on the subject I have to mention that I had planned to exclude any stories about Henry Ford from this book, along with Colonel Sanders, Coca Cola, Andrew Carnegie, McDonalds, Wrigleys, Woolworth, J C Penney, any American President or British Prime Minister, Emerson, Edison or Einstein. However, this is not possible, nor is it fair. For a while, I kept getting the feeling that the Americans were stealing an unfair lead in this race for human behavioural improvement and I wanted to shout out for the British way.

The thing was, the stories of success were so readily available from across the Atlantic. It was the American Andrew Carnegie, who gave his fellow American Napoleon Hill, the job of interviewing a massive amount of well known millionaires, to discover the common denominators in their success. Carnegie himself was a Scotsman. He was revered, respected and extremely wealthy. It was Carnegie who furnished Hill with letters of introduction. Without these letters Hill would not have got through many of the doors to get his interviews.

For me to have kept this book totally British, would have needed letters of introduction from someone like The Duke of Edinburgh to, Anita Roddick, Richard Branson, Alan Sugar, Eddie Shah, Sir Clive Sinclair, Sir Andrew Lloyd Webber, Paul McCartney, George Harrison, Ringo Starr, Mickie Most, and Elton John. I felt that these type of people were the modern counterparts in Great Britain, of the industrialists and inventors that Hill had interviewed all those years ago. It was not my goal for me to do that in this book, but I think an excellent idea for the future . . . Anyway, the fledgling American car industry used to close down for the Winter. People reckoned that you had to garage your car for the bad weather. This attitude reflected on sales, which slowed to a trickle. Year after year, it was noted that this trickle came from the same garage out in the Mid West. Henry Ford sent a top executive to find out why this dealership was selling cars in the Winter. The executive asked the owner, and the owner said that *he didn't know that you couldn't sell in the Winter*.

The owner of the garage saw no reason for not selling. If he had told himself that sales were not possible at this time of year, or gone into agreement with his fellow garage owners, the sales would not have occurred. *If you tell yourself that you like yourself, this liking of yourself will begin to help you*.

Compared to the American culture, we British seem humble. We don't like to shout off about our good points. The class system is still in place, and we have to behave a certain way if we are to be accepted by those in a certain strata. We are aware of vulgarity, but include newly acquired riches as vulgar, along

31

with loudness, saying good things about oneself, taking a positive viewpoint, and having a burning ambition.

The world has changed and we run the risk of being left behind, unless we begin to embrace the modern viewpoints that are helping other cultures make giant leaps forward. The Japanese have a fabulous outlook on industry. Many of the top firms in Japan treat employees as Family.

I was interested to see the progress made by Nissan, when they built a brand new car plant in my native North East of England. This was an area that had prospered on shipbuilding, and floundered when it could no longer stay competitive in the world market. The men were used to striking when a little more dialogue could have kept the ball rolling. The bosses were used to throwing their weight around without a care for the plight of the working man. The good news is that *the Nissan way is working here in England*, even though the general world recession has caused recent job losses.

New outlooks are beginning to creep into the boss/worker relationship. This will begin to percolate through into other industries. *We have to embrace other ideas from alien cultures, if we are to prosper in the world market*. We have to bolster our plans, preen our feathers, strut our stuff, shout our mouths off and tell the world that we like ourselves again, and we are ready to get back into the game.

You have to like the mistakes you have made.

They got you this far in life along with all the good moves. It is often the mistake that spawns the success. Learn from your mistakes. Treat them as an essential part of the lesson. Like and see the funny side of all those thoughts that you dread anyone ever finding out about. Enjoy the clumsiness, and like the time you broke your favourite cup. Don't you see, there is no point whatsoever in hating anything at all, and no space for embarrassment in anyone's life. Inability to confront anything, is a serious liability. If you have the choice between liking and hating, you may as well like.

People who like themselves are very attractive.

Did you think that liking yourself was a no go area? Are you so used to self criticism that you won't allow change? It's a funny thing, that as soon as you begin liking something, no matter how negative that thing or thought or person may be, it's charge begins to dissipate. Feel the pain disappear from an unpleasant memory, as soon as you see something good in that memory.

You are going to change the internal dialogue that goes on inside your head, for the better.

An unpleasant picture in your head, of a time when you fell to the ground from a swing and banged

33

your head . . . you remember the pain, the embarrassment, the bruise, staying off school the day you were
due to play on the football team for the first time . . .
you just have to find the good in that picture.

Before you say there can't be any good in such a
painful memory . . . was the sun shining? It was eh?
You remember the warmth on your cheek. And now
you remember how kind all of your friends were to
you, and the sweet smell of freshly mown grass. *Good*.
This works with any picture . . . any picture at all. What
would you rather focus on . . . the pleasure or the
pain? Find the good in the pain . . . no matter how
small that good is . . . find it and focus on it.

Maybe this concept of recording pictures in your
brain is new to you. This fact that you are making a
high quality movie of every single frame of your life
from birth and before, to now, is an actuality whether
you like it or not. But this kind of movie is different . . .
it hasn't been seen in the cinema . . . yet! This movie
contains smell, emotion, taste, likes and dislikes,
decisions and indecision.

Even better than all that, you can edit this movie
and get it to show just as you want it. *Special eh*?

Let's do a little exercise here. We need to use
something that we all know about and can relate to in
some way shape or form. I've got it.

I want you to get a picture in your mind, of a cow.
Read this paragraph over a few times to familiarize
yourself with what you have to do . . . then close your
eyes and make that picture appear in your mind. Do
you see that picture. Good, you see it. Make it a black

and white cow, and have it stand in a green field, all alone, chewing on some grass. The sky is blue and the sun is shining. Make the cow lie down. Make it get up. Now make it sing and dance . . . do that a few times, have a laugh watching the cow dance, and then make it disappear.

The first thing I want you to ask yourself, is who made that picture? *You made that picture*. Where was the picture? *It was in your mind*. Good, you placed that picture in your mind. Where is your mind? In your head. Could be. The head that makes up part of your body. I want you to understand right now that *you are not your body*, and *you are not your mind*. **You are you**.

You are a Being.

You use the brain to manifest a mental picture of what you the Being perceives, and you call this your mind. You house your mind in the brain, and the brain in your body. Then you try and forget the differences between you and your mind and your body, and you and the mind and the brain.

Pity these new babies didn't come complete with manuals eh? Can you imagine trying to work out a new computer software package without the manual? Well anyway, that is what we have to do if we are to work our way to the top of the heap. You have to put yourself out and find a workable way of liking yourself.

If you have a different viewpoint on **Human Being**, and that outlook is working for you, then unless you are in the business of studying the Psyche, stick with it. If you like the sound of my viewpoint then embrace it and see if it works for you. Life is more fun as a Spiritual Being, and I have known forever that I am exactly that. I have experienced past lives in detail. I have known other Planets and different forms of communication. I have experienced birth and death more times than I care to relate here in these pages.

I have reached a point, where I know that I am in command of my mind at any given time. I am the boss. I cannot imagine going through life thinking of myself as a meat body. I would then have to embrace the viewpoint of an animal. I would strive to survive. But as a Being playing the body game, a whole new philosophy comes into play . . . and there is no mystery to it!

I know some religions, or cults, that charge an eternity to unravel these secrets. They say that you have to do this, that and the other, and charge a zillion just to allow you on the first rung of their ladder.

I have news for you. You can start as high on the ladder as you wish. If you feel that your mind is sometimes in control of you, then you can try some commands that make you pop out on top again. Become a PAC Practitioner and use TTM. Try visiting my Paradise or discover your own. Try telling yourself to step out of your mind. Command yourself to be in command. Be aggressive if need be. Do whatever is necessary to stay in command at all times. Feeling good about anything ensures that you are more in control. There is no doubt about the fact that you can achieve far more in life as a happy person than you can as a miserable pessimist.

Have you ever heard about self talk?

That's right . . . talking to yourself. People used to be locked up in mental institutions for doing just that. Now you can buy books on the High Street about that subject alone. Many authors have written about the power of self talk. Some have turned it into an art form.

Did you know that your Sub Conscious Mind cannot tell the difference between fantasy and fact. *You can literally fool yourself to success*. Whatever you tell your Sub Conscious Mind, it will act upon. If you tell it that you like yourself, then it will believe you. If you tell it that you are successful, then it will do everything in it's power to turn that positive success suggestion, into a physical reality. If you tell it that you are stupid, then it will help prove you correct. This last paragraph of data is of such staggering importance, that I would like you to stop reading for a while and just think about it.

I spent a portion of my life erasing the stressful times from my memory, of this lifetime and others, and this worked to a degree. Even though it involved focusing on the negative, just to confront a previously unconfrontable memory, it did release attention units for further use.

I had thought that the Sub Conscious Mind only harboured negative things and I spent all of my time trying to erase them. When I occasionally succeeded that was fine, but I didn't command the Sub Conscious

Mind to do anything positive *for me*. I just treated it like some kind of negative presence. Now I know the truth, and sharing it with you is as exciting for me as first discovering it for myself.

The Sub Conscious Mind is the most powerful computer in the world. It does exactly as it is told. It works in the present tense and always as if it is, and you are, exactly as you have suggested.

Oh boy, now you can really get down to brass tacks. What are you going to do with this gem of wisdom? How are you going to harness the awesome power of the most formidable brain ever conceived. We all have one. What are you going to do with yours?

You must know that this Sub Conscious Mind, or SM, is very different to your Conscious Mind, or CM. You use your CM to run your every day life. You can hold one thought at a time in the CM. The CM has a fraction of the power that is contained in the SM. The SM is beavering away every minute of your life serving you as you have commanded it to serve. It is the SM that will give you inspiration, or sudden solutions to problems. This can often happen during TTM. Sometimes it will answer your question after you have forgotten what that question was. The SM likes time to work on your commands at it's leisure. How many times have you had a name on the tip of your tongue. An hour later it comes to you. That is the SM at work, constantly striving for success.

I picture my SM as a giant office with a huge storeroom full of files. I have an archive section, a microfilm section, a pending section, and a section for continuous action. Audio, visual, film, the feel department. It has everything I need and it's a beautiful place. There are computers everywhere and a large staff of very contented friends. My best friend in the office is my Secretary. When I want something from the SM, my Secretary always gets it for me.

I have a Messenger, and I use my Messenger to send messages to people and places. I have a Guardian who ensures that I am safe and sound at all times. My Guardian sometimes uses my Messenger and vice versa. They both have access to my Secretary. They all trust each other and I believe in them implicitly. They are all my best friends. I have deep faith in my SM and I treat my Helpers there with ultimate respect.

You must understand that I am not talking about any kind of magic here, when I say that the SM will get you into situations that are exactly right for what you want in life. The SM can see things that the CM cannot. Hunches are given to you routinely by the SM. You can bet your life that for every hunch that you are lucky enough to be given by your SM, it has worked overtime to get it for you. Your Secretary may have scoured millions of files, your Messenger could have journeyed on countless missions, and your Guardian would have been watching over these events all the while.

Consider this. You are looking for a special type of guitar for the new band that you have just joined. It's a pedal steel and you haven't ever been interested in such an instrument before. Next thing you know you're at a gig and there is a Country band playing. You talk in the dressing room afterwards and it transpires that the pedal steel player is just about to upgrade his guitar as he has just come in to some money. You buy the guitar that you said you wanted, there and then.

Now you were probably looking in the window of some Newsagent or other, and this gig may have been advertised. You weren't interested in Country Music gigs as you were looking to buy a kettle at the time. In fact you probably didn't see the advert at all. Your SM did though. It also noticed that the guitar player was selling his pedal steel. That was a separate advert. The SM linked them for you and suggested you go to the gig. The SM gave you the desire to attend a potentially beneficial event. It used this data gathered from a Newsagents window, in it's search for a possible answer to your predicament. To that degree . . . the SM is magic as we know it.

But when you consider your telepathic abilities, which we will discuss later . . . the fact that you could just attract the right situation by sending the SM *a light thought* concerning your requirements . . . well, we can call it magic-magic if you wish.

I can help you programme the SM.

Together we can get started on filling it so full of your present time dreams, that if you keep working at it, I guarantee your life will change for the better within twenty one days. Are you ready for this little baby then? Are you ready to tread where you probably have not been before?

The secret of self esteem, is in knowing how to inject yourself with as much of it as possible.

A very workable way is to make yourself a cassette tape of personalised affirmations. Play your favourite relaxing music in the background, as this seems to make the mind more open to your positive suggestions. A feeling of deep relaxation helps also.

This is what I want you to do right now. Read through my list. If these words of mine are good for you, then that will be a great start. Read them out aloud. Sing them. Have a bit of fun with them . . . but be serious about the outcome. Look in the mirror and get used to yourself. You are about to change your life for the better.

Put your favourite music on at a relaxing volume.

Make that music instrumental only. I love Bach's concerto number one for the violin in A minor. I go with the crescendos and emphasise my affirmations in different ways each time. I also like relaxing music that just drifts by me.

On my Audio Cassette Success Programme, I have used brand new music, which for me works well. This music was written especially for the purpose. If you can get a hold of this Audio Programme then it will help you understand the practice and theory of Self Talk. You may wish to make your tape more subliminal.

That is having the affirmations just too low for the CM to hear comfortably. I prefer to hear what is going on, as I like to be in total control as much of the time as possible. We let enough unwanted data slip into the SM as we stroll through life, without relinquishing control when we don't need to.

If you get on well with this idea, which does work well and is so easy to do, then I expect you to make up your own programme of personalised affirmations with your favourite music in the background. You can increase and decrease the volume as it suits you. You could even write and record your own music if you are that way inclined. The object is to get as much of *you* into this programme as is possible.

For now, relax and listen to some music, whilst reciting and emphasising my list of positive affirmations. This will get you used to the type of thing to say, sing, or chant. Once you have done this a few times, get yourself a cassette recorder and have some fun recording your own voice, with your favourite music playing in the background. Get used to hearing yourself. I know this is hard to begin with. I had to do it for the first time too. Now I love using my voice for affirmations. I enjoy hearing what I have to say, because I always tell myself good things.

This is not hypnosis. This is communicating with your Sub Conscious Mind. You are suggesting *internal dialogue* for the future. If you are going to have dialogue in your head, then you need to be in control of it. Every communication must be in the present tense. I'll use the first person singular to begin with, and then the third person singular. We use the first person, as that is the way we have grown used to talking to ourselves. We are also used to being told by others that we are a certain way, hence the third person. Always talk to yourself with the idea that what you want, or how you want to be, is already accomplished.

I call this part of the programme...

affirmations

talk to yourself and expect good results

1 I like myself I like myself I like myself
2 Life is good and getting better all the time
3 I am a good person
4 I enjoy my Family
5 I am clever
6 I am wise and hold my own counsel
7 I have a healthy body
8 I am the perfect weight for my height and build
9 I am honourable
10 Integrity is an important part of my life
11 I have a healthy way of living
12 I am tolerant and interested in other points of view
13 I am a good learner
14 I feel in harmony with my surroundings
15 I am in harmony with the world
16 I have a good sense of humour
17 I enjoy listening to people
18 I am in control of my mind

19 I feel powerful
20 I am willing to change a decision for a better view point
21 I love my Family
22 I am a creative person
23 I see my life in long term vision
24 I always have excess money to give away
25 I enjoy giving to others
26 I always go the extra mile
27 I give over and above what is required of me
28 Money seems to be attracted to me
29 I enjoy a feeling of inverse paranoia
30 The world is conspiring to do me good
31 Good things always seem to come my way
32 People just seem to like me
33 I am thought of as being good company
34 I always seem to do the right thing
35 I am gifted with determination
36 I always get what I want and others benefit along the way
37 I enjoy working towards the achievement of my goals
38 I like helping others
39 I learn something new every day
40 I am a high achiever
41 When I win my Family and friends win also
42 I am happy with myself
43 I am happy with the world
44 I enjoy my own company as well as other peoples'

1 You like yourself You like yourself You like yourself
2 Life is good and getting better all the time

3   You are a good person
4   You enjoy your Family
5   You are clever
6   You are wise and hold your own counsel
7   You have a healthy body
8   You are the perfect weight for your height and build
9   You are honourable
10 Integrity is an important part of your life
11 You have a healthy way of living
12 You are tolerant and interested in other points of view
13 You are a good learner
14 You feel in harmony with your surroundings
15 You are in harmony with the world
16 You have a good sense of humour
17 You enjoy listening to people
18 You are in control of your mind
19 You feel powerful
20 You are willing to change to a better view point
21 You love your Family
22 You are a creative person
23 You see your life in long term vision
24 You always have excess money to give away
25 You enjoy giving to others
26 You always go the extra mile
27 You give over and above what is required of you
28 Money seems to be attracted to you
29 You enjoy a feeling of inverse paranoia
30 The world is conspiring to do you good
31 Good things always seem to come your way
32 People just seem to like you

33 You are thought of as being good company
34 You always seem to do the right thing
35 You are gifted with determination
36 You always get what you want and others benefit too
37 You enjoy working towards the achievement of your goals
38 You like helping others
39 You learn something new every day
40 You are a high achiever
41 When you win your Family and friends win also
42 You are happy with yourself
43 You are happy with the world
44 You enjoy your own company as well as other peoples'

What do you think then? Did you feel stupid, or did you take to it like Martin Luther King to a microphone? I advise you to work on your affirmations every day. I have got myself to the point where I am automatically optimistic, happy, cheerful and ready for life.

I have to admit that in the beginning. . . dark old ways would impinge when I dropped my guard. That doesn't happen anymore. My frame of mind is exactly as I want it. Dynamic, and positively charged. I have my own data in the SM and it's working for *me*. As Leader of the PAC, I have come a long way towards a goal of a positive attitude at all times, but I am always ready to learn something new. My job as Leader is always on offer to an Advanced PAC Practitioner who has shown greater worthiness. We're moving on rapidly to more advanced stages, and I want you to thoroughly acknowledge yourself as a contender for my job. . . but there's a way to go yet.

You should realise also that affirmations can be used for short term gain too. You can make them up for specific day to day activities. You can also programme yourself each night before you sleep, to wake up cheerfully and optimistically at exactly. . . say 7am.

Don't try this. . . *trying is always trying*. . .you must have FAITH. *Just do it*! It is no good learning how to work the SM without ever working it. Put the alarm clock in another room, and tell yourself what time you want to wake up, and what mood you desire to wake up in.

What do people do once they know about the SM and CM? They like themselves enough, know about positive affirmations, and are taking responsibility for themselves? They have forgiven all and sundry for anything and everything?

They learn to unravel the age old secret of success.

A formula was made famous by Napoleon Hill in his book *Think and Grow Rich*. Hill said that the secret of great wealth would reveal itself at least once in every chapter of his book, and you would recognise it if you were ready for it. The other part of the formula would already be with you if you were ready for great riches.

47

I think we are ready to talk about

whatever you can hold in your mind...

stage three

whatever you can hold in your mind

> What the mind can conceive and believe, the
> mind can achieve... **Napoleon Hill**

Guglielmo Marconi told his friends that he believed
there was a way of sending human voices through
the air without the aid of wires. They thought he was
nuts, and took him to be psycho analysed. He proved
himself correct of course, by inventing wireless
telegraphy.

*Do you believe in telepathy? Do you think it is
possible to hold a picture in your mind, and have
someone else tune in to that picture?*

If you do believe this, then how can it benefit you?
We are learning how to use the magnificent power of
the SM, and not how to defend ourselves from it.

You can't ever win by defending!

*Telepathy works, and exists as a phenomena, **to be
used**.*

How many times has someone called you, and the
first thing you say to them is that you were just
thinking about them. It happens between my wife
and I often. She'll say something to me and I'll tell her
that I was thinking of that item 45 seconds prior. I

have been known to answer her and she'll turn around and tell me that she hadn't verbalised the question. . . it was merely a thought in her head.

I had the ability to know the time within a minute or so. I didn't own a watch as I felt they were uncomfortable around the wrist, but I always knew the time. It became a bit of a party trick after a while. Then I decided, for whatever reason, to lick my consideration about watches being uncomfortable. I bought a new watch and lost the ability to tell the time for myself. When I decide that I want that ability back however, I'll ditch the watch and that ability will return to me.

It is beyond comprehension, that this most magnificent creation we call Human Being, which uses the most sophisticated computer ever made as it's operation base, would leave out a simple communication process like telepathy from it's software package.

Can you imagine buying a computer that couldn't talk to a printer?

A human being, without the ability to transfer the contents of it's mind, or brain, to the physical universe, is a cruel idea. Show yourself pictures of a fabulous holiday destination, and then tell yourself that you can't go there. Cruel isn't it?

Thank goodness we have the ability to hold a picture, or an idea, in our minds, and then have it become a physical reality!

This is an ability which needs to be used. You need to practice. You have to decide what you want. Mock that picture up in your head and give it life. Charge it with emotion and faith, love and sex, desire and yearning.

The demands that you place on your SM must be combined with liberal mixtures of FAITH and STRONG EMOTION!

This is how the SM works...the command and the feelings...the SM loves the feelings...*feelings* ...**FAITH**,,, desire///how exhilarated you will feel with this accomplishment\\/*the* **LOVE** *and the* **SEX** *that go* with the desire anD:::yearNING./././ NB NB NB.

Demand the physical existence of whatever it is you want. If it is money...see the cash...look at the currency...and touch those banknotes in your head just as easily as if they were on a table in front of you. **Get the feelings**! See what service you are willing to offer in exchange for that cash, and at the same time see the joy that this money will bring you.

Mix emotion with desire, formulate a plan, mix the ingredients together, then go and make it happen.

You are in charge! A person without a plan can only drift with the tide and be the effect of other peoples' desires. The stronger the plan, the bigger the engine. Big engines take on fast currents. Big engines and big plans, get you where you want to be.

You have to visualise what it is you want, before it will happen!

You don't build a house without plans. Can you imagine telling a builder to erect a house for you with four bedrooms and two reception rooms. You couldn't complain when you viewed the finished product for the first time and discovered that the house didn't have a garage or a bathroom. You didn't tell the builder!

A movie director would never dream of ordering a song for a scene without briefing the songwriter . . . or better still showing the songwriter the scene. Can you imagine a heavy metal discordant bash accompanying a sweet love scene, or an Irish Country Jig playing merrily as a cat got run over by a car.

The order that you place has to be accurate.

Tell life what you want and it will obey!

Visualise the finished outcome of your plan, and attach yourself to the sort of contacts and friends who will be most beneficial to your achievement of good and fast results. Your mental pictures have to be as detailed as those house plans should have been. That car you want to own has to have a colour and an engine. The house has to have a location and a view.

WHATEVER YOU CAN HOLD IN YOUR MIND

The girl has blue eyes or brown hair. That man in your life has ambition as well as looks...what kind of ambition? Who sells those cars? How can you connect up to those people who can help you get where you want to go?

We did a little exercise with a cow in a field. Remember? That illustration is an important part of this programme. It has shown that you have the ability to change pictures around in your head. You can change your plans...you can change the colour of that car you desire. You can change course mid stream if you think that you are making a mistake.

You are in charge and you make the decisions.

You enlist the help of your Sub Conscious Mind, by telling it what you want to do, and then letting it get on with the accomplishment of it's task. You have a servant, and you need to learn how to get the most from that *service*.

We can illustrate the power of the SM with the help of a Teddy Bear. Sit the Teddy on a chair, and then decide that the Teddy will move onto the floor. Once you have made that decision, move the Teddy onto the floor. You saw that action through from the decision to the final outcome using the CM. If you hadn't have been able to use the CM, the SM would have taken over and made plans for the removal of the Teddy as you desired. You would have probably left the room, only to return an hour later and move

53

the Teddy without even thinking about it. You may have said to one of your children that the Teddy should be in a bedroom and would they move it. The reply may be reasonable. The child may say that it isn't doing any harm and you don't usually complain. . .it's not your usual seat anyway. You see, you have put the SM into action and it will serve you well. . .if you programme it well. I often think of it like a tapeworm when it isn't programmed properly, because it has the apparency of being stupid enough, to kill you, yet it just does as it is told.

Whatever you can hold in your mind you can have. . .so let's get the picture just right. Drawing onto paper can help. Writing out your goals for the world to see is essential. Formulating a plan on paper and continuously redrafting it until it is perfect is highly desirable.

Use your imagination.

You have two types, and it is this imagination that sets us apart from the competition. Your **Secondary Imagination**, is your ability to get ideas from what you can see. . .from things and ideas that have already been created. It is likely that this **Secondary Imagination** is working for you. . .and you are making it work for you, every day of your life.

Premier Imagination is that which is used to pluck an idea from "thin air". **Premier Imagination** is your link to the **ETHER WAVES**.

The total sum of everything ever thought is

available to you in the **ETHER WAVES**. The intelligence of others is available to you in the **ETHER WAVES**.

IT IS POSSIBLE TO CREATE SOMETHING FROM NOTHING *and have a totally original idea*.

It is also possible to apparently create something from nothing by tuning in to the **ETHER WAVES**.

Telepathy between minds is possible through this medium.

Premier Imagination is the most exciting faculty available to you...it will provide you with hunches and plans, ideas and creations, success *and* misery, total failure, dejection and insolvency. For it is your **Premier Imagination** which obeys your every whim and caprice. It is this PI that lies within your SM, awaiting instruction. It needs to be used, and you need to put it to work for you right now. Don't be shy. Have FAITH and use your **Premier Imagination** to guide you on your route to *success*.

Don't forget that you have to tell it what to do. PI will guide you to *hell* if that is what you are telling it to do. If you tell it that "life is hard", "it's an uphill struggle", "I can't do that", or anything at all negative, it will make that happen just as sure as "eggs is eggs".

Just you take the time right now to once again look over my *Positive Affirmations* in Stage Two, and you may find that you now have a greater understanding of WHY they are used.

You have to keep injecting the SM with *positive*

commands for the PI to get working on making you successful. The PI is waiting for instruction...don't let it latch on to some casual thought or doubt that you may have allowed to lightly slip through.

Never ever ever drop your guard!

Let your *positive commands* be the dominant force, for **the PI *will go to work on making your thoughts a reality***.

Check your course and trim your sails. Are you heading in the right direction. Do you have the correct charts? If you changed some points of your plan a little, would that speed up the accomplishment of your goal. Have you thoroughly acknowledged your **Premier Imagination**, or are you in doubt.

You can have FAITH...or you can be FAITHLESS.

Your success begins with FAITH in your ability to achieve it. You must have FAITH in every constituent part of your route to success. FAITH that forgiveness has set you on your way. FAITH, that by filling your head so full of **POSITIVITY** that there is no alternative but to succeed. FAITH in your ability to like yourself and others. FAITH in the PAC. FAITH in **Premier Imagination**. FAITH in the SM. FAITH in your chosen route and FAITH in your *actions*.

There is no room for cynicism as this only produces cynicism. No space for duplicity for this is not straightforward. I am leading you on course for true success. I am not talking about transient success. I am dealing in true success.

Whenever I talk to people about goals I always encourage them to plan their lives with as much naivety as possible to begin with.

Do not qualify your goals!

When you are first discovering what your goals are, just let them flow out. Ask yourself the right questions. This is a powerful piece of data. Good questioning of yourself will stimulate the right answers.

If you could have anything in the world, what would it be?

If you had millions of pounds, what would you do with it?

If you could have any one good quality that you have observed in someone else, what is that quality?

If you could choose your job, what would you do for a living?

On January 2nd 1993, I was at a new year plus one party when I bumped into an old friend of mine. I complained to him that I was just about to start another musical venture, and that I saw it as an uphill struggle.

How could something turn out easy with that kind of visualisation?

I told him that my previous product had not sold well, and how hard it was to contemplate something new so soon after failure. We had both studied the subject of goals for sometime in the past, but my interest had sadly declined as I became more and more active in the music business. His interest however had increased, as it had a direct relationship with his business.

He asked me what I would like as an epitaph. Quick as a flash I replied, Phil Murray wrote good songs. His reply was that I had already accomplished that.

That was the trigger for me. He pushed the right button.

I had so many realisations in one instant, that my life was literally transformed there and then. I looked at my plans for the previous four products that I had on the marketplace. I'd had no strategy whatsoever for the sale of the product.

I was elated to know why I had failed with these products, and I began to succeed from that moment onwards!

I quickly looked back at what had happened.

All the plans that I had made for the products had worked, but I had ultimately failed. I'd dreamed up the ventures, started my own record and publishing companies, enlisted the help of the musicians that I needed, wrote the songs . . . had the covers designed and the compact discs and cassettes manufactured. I signed my company to a major distribution deal and released the recordings . . . the reviews were excellent and I was proud of the products as I still am.

The products failed in the marketplace at that time, because my plan did not extend to sales.

I had not thought the magic thoughts to do with sales.

In fact it was worse than that, because my outlook had actually taken the form of not being interested in the financial aspect of my work. That would be someone else's job... *but I didn't give anyone else the job*!

I was able to see exactly where I went wrong in a split second, when I remembered just what my goal had been for these products. "Phil Murray songs will always get released because they are excellent songs." Sure enough they are. Nothing about records selling in massive quantities and bringing enjoyment to those who bought them. I had done a lot of work, but my plan had been inconclusive. I had not visualised the final outcome as sales. I had swallowed the cliches about artistes and money, and did not want my art tainted with finance.

I do now! Taint me! Taint me!

What good is a great song if no one hears it? Great songs do not pay the mortgage unless they sell. Do you see? The viewpoint must be positive and detailed at every stage.

I recently asked the exact same "epitaph" question to a friend of mine who was having trouble deciding what to do with the rest of her life. She didn't like the question so I changed it a little to, "after you die, how would you like to be remembered"? She replied that she would feel pompous expecting anyone to remember her for anything.

59

She of course will have to take care to do nothing of any note at any point in her life, in the hope that her expectation be realised.

Actually, it was a modest viewpoint that she had but really there is nothing wrong at all with talking about goals and aspirations...to the right people. Beware of small mindedness. Beware of people that tell you that your plans are too ambitious, or that you are, "too big for your boots". If someone criticises you, examine their own track record. Are they being helpful or envious. Do they talk in positives or negatives. Are they looking forward to the rest of their lives, or do they see it as an uphill struggle with no guarantee of success.

You will attract like minded people through telepathy. Other people tune in to the **ETHER WAVES**. *Premier Imagination* will home in on other people's thoughts if those thoughts are attractive. Make sure that you are holding the right thoughts in your head. You don't want to attract the wrong events or people into your life.

You cannot afford to punish yourself with negative thoughts.

Think of your head as a garden. Grow beautiful flowers and frequently weed it! It isn't good enough to just plant the seed. Think about this gardening point of view just for a moment. If you just left the seed on top of the soil, it would probably get strangled by weeds...just like an idea. You plant eed according to the instructions, and then you water it regularly. You prune as needed. You feed the young plant. You check for bugs. If you have been successful, you will be able look at the wonderful flowers in the Summer or harvest the fruit in the autumn.

Getting the idea is great. Making the decision is great. Formulating the plan is great...

Advanced PAC Practitioners always get into Action.

They never let an idea slip by without action. They trust **Premier Imagination.** They know that this principle of success can only work with action. A company may manufacture the finest sailing boat the world has ever seen, but the Chairman of that company must know that the product has to be sold, if the initial idea is to be ultimately successful. Advanced PAC Practitioners know that action must be carried on all the way down the line to the logical conclusion of the initial idea.

Postulate sales...if sales are what you want!

I shudder to think how many truly beautiful songs there are, lying around in someone's bedroom in demo form, unavailable to the world. The dream must have been within the songwriter to begin with. They must have had a positive attitude and let the

61

negative attitude slip through the back door. It's you choice...PA or NA. The latter is a swear word in m' home. I have taught my children to challenge me at an' time they feel that I am criticising them destructively And they do! Occasionally of course, it has been know for them to throw down the challenge to hide the fac that they have just done something they felt the should not have done. But, on the whole, it works. Whe I hear the words, "Dad, is that destructive criticism?" always check myself. If it is, I apologise.

You see, I think that there are few things on eartl worse than continuously challenging a child's view point. Or telling that child that he or she is alway wrong. Or convincing children they are stupid, o horrible, or small, or not wanted. Laughing at thei mispronunciations or exclaiming surprise that the didn't know something that hasn't even found it's wa into the Encyclopedia Britannica yet!

This attitude does no good. The SM is workin overtime in young children and serving them wel Every time that it is called stupid, it goes on to prov that self fulfilling prophecy correct.

Ban NA and Destructive Criticism from your lives!

This will aid every aspect of your existence, an certainly stop any thoughts entering your head abou giving up...or this is just too hard...or even h couldn't do it...maybe next time...it's just not m day...I wasn't cut out for it anyway.

Just as the idea has to be right, it's execution must be thorough also. With NA kept at bay, as you proceed on your path to success, the SM will present you with answers, hunches, long shots and sure fire certainties. You must not sit back when there are things to be done.

It's time to assemble your Supergroup.

There is no such thing as a one man band. Everyone needs someone at some time. Even if the one man band plays his own songs, he still needs an audience. His influences must have come from somewhere and he still needs other people in order to exist.

We all need other people, and that is one of the joys of life.

I have been in the music business all of my life. I remember, during a particularly successful period of my career in music, going back to the North East and meeting an old school pal. He was a guitar player in a working band, and he invited me to the gig that night. I sang a few numbers with them, and then my friend handed me a demo tape and asked me to try and get them a deal. I played it to my manager when I returned home, and he got them a deal almost immediately, with a record company that I had been signed to in the past.

Their first record was a hit!

Do you know how statistically hard it is to get a hit? In some countries it was number one! Does anyone

63

know the exact recipe for a hit song in an ever changing marketplace? I *know this much, it has little or nothing to do with the song.*

When the record entered the charts, word went round that the drummer wasn't up to it. I said that his drumming had got them a hit. "Anyone can drum," was the answer. "And get a hit?" I replied.

The drummer was paid off.

The song was at number five in the British chart when the first mutterings could be heard about the sax player. "He only plays sax," I could hear. "Have you seen him on stage?" I replied. "Sax playing is just an overdub, we can get someone in just for the records." "But he's good fun and adds sparkle," replied.

The sax player went the journey.

The studio was booked for the next recording. Someone said that the bass player couldn't play slap bass. "But the band don't have the slap bass style," replied. "Yes, but Rod Stewart's bass player is available for the session". "But the bass player has been with the band forever," I replied, "and he's good."

Goodbye to the bassist, and the piano player for good measure.

Now the two songwriters were left . . . my pal the guitarist, and the singer. The two follow up releases had flopped. "It's only the voice that people hear," was the phrase of that moment. "But the guitarist is one of the best I've ever heard and he's my friend," replied. "The singer can write with anyone, and we can get him a solo deal in the States," I heard.

Before the singer actually went solo, he offered my friend the guitarist a smaller percentage on their writing partnership...him being the singer and all that...the guitarist walked away, and we all said goodbye to a fine band.

It was the group members *and* their attitudes that made up the band. *The magic merging of the people.* Not just the individual performances brought together. The minds together caused the positive vibes. A "success waiting to happen" occurs with alignment of peoples' goals. People tune into the same wavelength and walk the path together. They contribute to the master plan in different ways. A half way decent drummer may be the heart and soul of the band. There may be better drummers...but does a drummer just drum?

The goals have to be tuned and honed, careful plans have to be made, and *action must occur*.

How many times have the Beatles been discussed after dinner. What a lucky break for Ringo. That George was just along for the ride. John writes better on his own. It was Paul's looks. George Martin showed them the chords you know.

I always thought that it was the five of them TOGETHER!

I always saw the creative team as having five

65

members. The magic occurred between them. 1 + + 1 + 1 + 1 = 75. The phenomena was the group. You could say that you liked John the best. . . but that didn't make him the main reason for their phenomenal success and group talent.

I worked with a famous producer for a while. I learnt many things from him, but the main thing was the viewpoint he held about his role. He viewed himself as a catalyst. He called himself the communication point for the group, and asked that all ideas be channelled through him.

Our drummer thought he was rubbish and told him so. This producer also owned the record company we were signed to. The producer told the drummer that he could take over. The drummer later apologised when no more studio time was forthcoming from the record company. The point is, that his role was not acknowledged, and, as it happens, we needed him, because he was *part of the formula*.

Now is the time to form your Supergroup

You will need a **Nuclear Supergroup** and an **Extended Supergroup**. The **Nuclear Supergroup** will comprise of the people necessary for the smooth and expansive running of your life. You will head this group whether you are a leader or not. Next will be your spouse and children. Then the remainder of your Family will fit around your plans as you desire. Also there are your employees, or workmates, or bosses, or colleagues.

Now we will work on the *Extended Supergroup*. **Can you see that when two people get together with a common purpose, a third force is created?** Not only do you have your own viewpoint, and that of your colleague, but you also have the third force, which is the result of the combination of the two viewpoints.

$$1 + 1 = 3.$$

Now is the time to assemble the team who will make up your Supergroup. Naturally, a team of Advanced PAC Practitioners is highly desirable, but we must always remember that it is the goal that is important here. It could be that the most miserable person in existence just happens to be the contact with the formula for the accomplishment of the next stage of your goal. I certainly wouldn't let such a person into my Supergroup, but I would certainly develop a relationship with him...and I would let him in to a branch of my Supergroup.

The Nucleus of my *Extended Supergroup*, comprises of Advanced PAC Practitioners only. My wife is in my *Extended Supergroup* as well as in the Nuclear. That decision will be up to you. Different marriages and relationships work in a variety of ways. I have a friend who's business is totally unrelated to mine, but our common ground is PAC membership. He is in my *Extended Supergroup*, which presently has a membership of 5. I aim for 10 as full membership.

Unless you are very fortunate indeed, you will find that membership is not necessarily permanent, although in an ideal world it would be.

The purpose of the *Extended Supergroup* is to help it's members. The Group must meet regularly, and agree to it's own success. You may take your problems to these meetings and have them solved. You should expect contacts to be forthcoming. If you have a wealthy member, then perhaps you can arrange for this member to finance your loan requirements, rather than take them outside of your Group.

The Extended Supergroup is an interdependent entity.

Don't forget that you have to give to this group. It will be as strong as it has *giving members*. But it's principle lies within the equation $1 + 1 = 3$. You will have access to brains that are not in your head. Different combinations will provide different solutions. Advanced PAC Practitioners, by their very definition, always succeed, and a group of pooled resources from such a group will be awesome. Use this data as soon as possible and get your Supergroup together. Don't dump rubbish on this group. Do what you can for yourself. Respect a member's privacy. Build on mutual understanding and common ground.

Jot down the names of twenty people that you would consider for group membership. Next to each name, write the reason why you like them in your group. Whittle the candidates down to a manageable ten. Casually begin to discuss your ideas for such a venture with each candidate. You could strike lucky and have someone turn around to you right away and say what a good idea you have just presented them with. You may have to start again from scratch. Begin now. If you feel that this idea has merit . . . have FAITH and get into action!

This is one more step on your road to personal success.

I am telling you right here and now to be your own insurer. Guarantee your own success right now. Go on . . . make the decision to be successful in whatever is your desire. Be excited. Assemble your Supergroup. Banish NA and destructive criticism from your life.

Get the picture of your goal just how you want it, and hold that idea and plan in your mind until it becomes a physical reality.

Don't ever be afraid to own money, because

money brings joy to the enlightened . . .

stage four

money brings joy to the enlightened

. . . riches begin in the mind . . .   *Phil Murray*

You cannot escape the fact that you need money in this world. We have designed the game in such a way that money is absolutely essential. We throw ourselves awkward curves by making certain aspects of money not politically correct. Or, if one has more money than another we are told not to flaunt it.

We have shrouded money with mystery and fabricated lies about it. Lies like, "you cannot be artistic, and into money as well". The biggest misquote of them all . . . "money is the root of all evil". "The best things in life are free". "Money isn't everything" . . . [an excuse for not having *any*!] "Spiritual people don't need money". "Friendships and money just don't mix".

Do you want to know what I say?

Give me the cash!

Give me the cash in any currency that buys what I want. Hand me the money! Dish the dosh! Put the money on the table. Let's talk in financial terms.

Dollars, Pounds and Deutschmarks!

I can see cases full of the stuff. I make my £50 notes

into a wedge and carry them on my hip. I've got loads of money.

It's a rich man's world and I'm a rich man!

Get the picture. . . literally. Let's put the myth to rest that there is anything vulgar whatsoever about money.

Money is an exchange.

Before money, people traded possessions directly. All we have done is put money in the middle of that exchange. You sell something and take money for it, until you know what you want to spend that money on, and then you pass the money to the owner of whatever that thing is that you want to buy. Money itself is worthless. It is the agreements we have made about money that are valuable.

Money is not powerful. . . it's helpless. It *needs you to give it a purpose.*

It needs help in deciding what to do with itself. You can decide to use people's considerations about money to make yourself look powerful, but that is just a quick fix. We are after long term personal success in every aspect of our lives.

Let's make one thing quite clear. . . there is so much money in the world it's incredible. There are zillions of units of money out there and we call them all sorts of names. There are dollars and pounds, marks and lire, schillings and punts, drachmas and sheckels. . .it's all there for your taking.

All you have to do is provide a service that is needed or wanted, and someone will give you money in direct proportion to the grade of service you supply. If you want lots of money, then you have to make sure you give service that people willingly pay dear for.

It is no good postulating a vast fortune for yourself, then taking a job as a waiter until it shows up. You can visualise yourself as the best waiter who ever lived, but history has shown that this job does not yield as well as, say, accountancy or being a film star.

Getting into full action mode, means action in the right direction.

So, we are getting money in perspective. We are agreed on the fact that you need money in order to live in this world, and we know about visualising.

Visualise yourself with lots of money.

Riches begin in the mind!

Decide exactly how much you want, and picture yourself already in possession of that money. Have FAITH in your visualisation. Decide on the currency and give yourself a time limit. Be firm. **Life will give you exactly what you demand of it**. Learn from my mistakes. I produced and manufactured for four years without a good financial return as one of the goals.

Money in the main, is a by-product of a goal. It would be quite correct to set yourself a goal and then have the money come in as a result of achieving that goal. For instance, you could decide that you wanted to invent the shirt that does not need to be washed. That is your goal. You bet your life, or your shirt, that when you achieve that goal, if you market the product properly, you will end up a wealthy person. If you feel that the cash is not a good thing for you to have, then you will probably sell the idea to someone else who is ready to enjoy the cash that will come from it.

I believe the Coca Cola recipe was sold for a few hundred dollars and that is a good example. You see, it wasn't sufficient to dream up the recipe. An ingredient was missing to make Coca Cola the phenomena that it is. The person who bought the recipe had that missing ingredient. He visualised the next step of the Coca Cola phenomena. . . *and put it into practice*!

If however, you find yourself without any goals whatsoever except a burning desire for cash, then there is no reason at all why you shouldn't copy someone else's success.

What earns money for one, can earn money for another!

73

Find an idea or a person, with a proven record of success. You can bet your life that any success has had it's trials and tribulations, and there is no reason at all why mistakes should have to be made twice. You have already learned from my expensive lesson that if you want money, you should always make it a part of your visualisation process. So if you want to own a launderette, and you site it on an estate where everyone owns their own washing machine, and John, your mate from the pub had already tried one there and gone bust, you must not be surprised if you struggle.

What I am telling you to do is copy success.

You have seen this happen in the music business. The Beatles came along and spawned a thousand imitators. Some of these groups that copied were absolutely excellent. Some used the Beatles as inspiration only, some copied the chord progressions and the harmonies. Some had managers that copied their manager.

You can see this copying in manufacturing. The Sony Walkman generated an awful lot of imitations. Car styles are copied. Firms let rivals try a product out in the marketplace before committing themselves and their cash to a similar product. *There are trend-setters, and trend followers.* **Both systems can make you vast sums of money**!

If you want lots of cash, find someone

who is already making lots of cash, and in the absence of any other goal of your own, copy them.

If you want to hold on to your money, it seems to be a good idea to always keep 10% for yourself. Whatever money comes in, just take 10% straight off the top, and keep it in the bank, building society or some other sure fire, safe place. ***Make your money reproduce itself***. Let someone give you more money for letting them look after your money for you.

On no account must you ever spend this money!

This is your estate and security. You will even find that some people want to give you more money just because you own money. Just let this money gather momentum of it's own accord, and give you a feeling of security.

Money gives you the luxury of being able to say no, and hold out for better deals. Without money, you run the risk of taking the first offer that comes along out of desperation.

I doubt there is a self-made millionaire in existence who has not, and does not, borrow.

Now I have to be careful in what I say here. I don't want to give the impression that you can *just* borrow to make yourself rich. I am talking about using other peoples' money as an aid to the execution of a worthy goal. I don't support borrowing for the sake of it. *The goal comes first.* But I'll tell you this . . .

Borrowing is the Capitalist way.

The industry of Great Britain and indeed the rest of the world, exists because it's founders were able to borrow. There is always money available for a good practical idea. If you have your goal well visualised, written out and planned in fine detail, and you get into full action mode, you will get all of the money you need, if the person you are dealing with can see the validity of your plan. *If not, then you need to find the financier who is looking for your plan.*

The Bible states that, *love* of money is the root of all evil . . . greeding and lusting and worshipping the stuff is my interpretation of that line. George Bernard Shaw said that *lack* of money is the root of all evil. We must be clear on the fact that money itself is nothing at all. It is merely significance. Focus on the good things that can be accomplished with money . . . the building of Schools and Hospitals . . . the furtherance of brilliant ideas.

You will definitely need money, and an Advanced PAC Practitioner has no problems both getting, and holding on to money. You may need some cash from elsewhere to get started. As long as your plans are sound and your purpose honourable, borrow at the lowest rate possible, from the highest profile institution of good repute, and preferably on personal recommendation from more than one source.

Premier Imagination will help you get the money you need.

You have to remember that there are people out there who's sole purpose of employment is to find places to put a client's money. There are fund managers out there looking to get rid of some money. You have to link up. There is nothing more heartening to a well balanced fund manager with excess cash, than to be presented enthusiastically with a sound idea, and a request for financial assistance with which to fulfil that idea.

Don't fight the financial system . . . use it.

Be wise in your borrowing. Look for the very best terms, and never be afraid to question even the highest profile outfit on the High Street, to see if you can improve on those terms. I have saved so much money during my life, just through the wise use of words. My wife is also well versed in the art of presenting her case for financial gain. As long as everyone wins, I actually feel I am performing a service to the person with whom I am haggling.

Many, many years ago, my wife and I went shopping for a jacket each in London. We had a budget of £100 each. I quickly found one that suited me fine and bought it within the budget. Next door there was a jacket that my wife fell in love with. It was £120. We looked at each other knowingly, and entered the shop. I told the owner that our budget was £100 but the jacket that we liked in his window was £120, would he mind reducing it to £100. He asked if we would mind increasing our budget to £120 and laughed at us. We bandied words for a while, but I knew the mark up on this jacket would be in the region of 100%, *so I felt good about giving him the profit that he would still be getting if he sold us the jacket for* £100.

He sold it to us for £100, and it was a fair deal for all involved.

You have to be able to ride the waves when you try for good prices. I saw a studio quality cassette recorder that had been reduced from £800 down to £400. I asked the assistant why, and he told me that it had been in the showroom for two years, and they had used it to sell from stock. This was now the last one, and they were discontinuing that particular player.

I knew they were selling it at cost price, but I also knew that they had already made huge profits on it during the two years that it had served them well. I asked for the manager, and offered him £200, with an accompanying explanation. He laughed at me. I rode the wave. He wasn't used to selling beneath what an item had cost, and I was introducing him to the idea that he had actually already made his money on the product. I felt that I was offering a fair deal that offered each party a gain.

He sold it to me for £200.

Whenever I went into the shop after that, he *expected* to give me a good deal. We did lots of business together.

You see, my goal is not to, "get one over on someone"...or, "screw them into the ground"...and I expect that attitude of mine to reflect back onto me. My goal is to win, and I believe that it is always possible for the other person to win at the same time.

I call this my win for all ingredient.

We had a mortgage with a building society, who we discovered were charging us 1% above the normal interest rate, because that particular house had the right to semi commercial use. It was a year before I realised this. I telephoned the company and spoke to the manager. I told him that I didn't want to pay the extra, and what's more, I *wanted the overpayment refunded*. He laughed, but I rode the wave. We talked some more, and he agreed to the reduction back down to domestic rate...*and to the refund*! He didn't want to lose my custom and he saw that I had a good case...I stayed with them for many years.

It is wise to adopt good selling techniques when buying.

A conversational approach works well...and getting on the same wavelength as the person you are dealing with is essential. Visualisation of the desired final result being already accomplished, is necessary, and slight mimicry is also a proven part of the formula.

Don't alienate yourself from someone by being too different. Find out what that person is aspiring towards...and *be* it. If he likes football...talk football. If you see that he's keen on something, and you don't have a clue, say that you had always wanted to know more about that something and let him explain. If you have a general interest in life with a Positive Attitude, it will always be true that you do want to know about something of which you are presently ignorant.

Physical mimicry works, but can sometimes be too obvious. You have to be subtle. If you talk like Prince Charles, and you're trying to sell to Paul Gascoigne, it may help to tone the upper class accent down a little...unless your customer is aspiring towards your style of speech. If he scratches his nose, you have to be able to scratch yours without really thinking about it. Those thoughts in the CM are telepathic too, and dependant on the awareness of the person you are with, he could tune in and feel that you are being facetious...to put it politely.

This is an honourable way of doing business, just like it would be if you learnt German to do business with a customer who spoke German.

A simple warning will suffice for any unscrupulous individuals who find themselves in possession of this book, and the powerful data contained herein. Firstly, I doubt if it is possible for you to absorb the finer points without an accompanying honourable purpose. But secondly, and more importantly, don't try and do anything other than good with this new technology . . . *it is all based on the fact of life that what you give you get!* **Whatever you put out will return just like a boomerang** . . .

This data, used for a dishonourable purpose, will destroy you!

You must have a good ethical code of conduct, and it must always take precedence over any scheme you may be contemplating that has a question mark attached to it. Refer to your ethical code, and trust it. Don't ever compromise with what you feel is correct.

Your ethical code needs to be reviewed frequently. It is a well known fact that people only do things that they think are *right*. Criminals don't rob, deceive and kill because they think it's wrong. They think that it is *right for them*. Surveys have shown that when people first come into contact with crime they feel an abhorrence. After they have taken part in criminal activity, they feel uncomfortable . . . when they have been around crime and criminals for a length of time, *it feels right*. You need to make your money honestly.

Your SM needs to be around powerful, ethically correct stimuli.

Another good financial idea is to give some of your cash away to make room for a new influx. Keep money flowing. Give to charity. When everyone else donates a pound, you should make it your business to give three! Find that organisation you enjoy giving to.

It's easier being spiritual with a pound in your pocket, *than it is on an empty stomach*!

Once money begins to flow your way, you must always remember that you are merely playing a game in the physical world. Do not let that game take over just because you are winning at it. This is the time to invest in the world that you really belong to. Let your money give you the time to study and discover more about the real you.

Read what the great prophets have had to say through the ages. There are some terrific ideas out there for the pondering. The idea of Karma...what you give you get...or doing to others only those things that you would not mind others doing to yourself. You sow what you reap. **You are what you think you are.**

The greater quantity of good inspirational material you read, the more able you will be to absorb new ideas and philosophies...and the easier your path to profit will be. When you find an author you like, look out for his or her recommendations. Does the book have a bibliography for further reading? If so, don't just read it...go and get the books it recommends and continue your progress.

Do you need specific books for your business? Do you have the manuals necessary for the smooth operation of your machinery. Do you feel good about giving specific books as presents to employees... or employers?

Do you waste time watching TV? Do you realise the TV is constantly on in the background? Do you go down to the Pub when you should be hard at work travelling your route to great wealth? *You have to put in the necessary hours, **in order to succeed***. Part of this work is reading and researching.

You can search deeply or superficially. The more spiritual you are in your outlook, the fuller your physical life will be. Play the body game to it's highest level of enjoyment, but always remember that when the game of life is up, *you* will still exist... answerable to yourself. Use this knowledge to enjoy yourself even more. This knowledge isn't a threat. It's an invitation to the party. A few rules and guidelines to help you achieve fulfillment. And in this picture that I am painting, always remember that there is nothing wrong with borrowing cash, or owning cash... just put it to good use!

You've got money, you're operating on a physical and a spiritual plane, you're a kind and forgiving person, you like yourself and others, you have goals... let me ask you this,

who is in charge now... you or your mind?

stage five

who is in charge now...you or your mind

> ...you do not need to be an electronic engineer, or a physicist, to operate your own servo-mechanism, any more than you have to be able to engineer an automobile in order to drive one, or become an electrical engineer in order to turn on the light in your room...   *Maxwell Maltz*

By now, you should be feeling the power that is yours to keep. There should be fullness of purpose at the forefront of your mind, and you should know who is in charge. If there are any old habits that are left over from the old you, then it may be an idea to put some attention on changing them for the better. If you have not changed any of the old considerations that may have been holding you back, then do it now.

You may have some physical problems that are hanging you up. You must do your best to get yourself into shape.

Get yourself into fully fit mode.

If you are planning to enjoy success fully, it is wise to have your body in a healthy state. I'm not talking about anything unreal here. I'm not suggesting that a bank clerk needs to be as fit as an athlete, or a fireman needing the strength of an ox.

You need to be fit enough for the lifestyle you are contemplating.

If you would like to give up smoking for instance, then I suggest that you give smoking an undesirable image. Tell yourself that you have a healthy body, and get a picture in your head of that undesirable image every time you want to smoke. If there is a type of behaviour that you do not enjoy in people, associate that behaviour with smoking. Smell an ashtray. Visit a patient who has just had a lung removed. Confront the phlegm that patient is coughing up. Check your teeth for nicotine stains.

All the time you are focusing on the negative, you are doing it from a positive point of view. If your sense of smell has suffered, aspire towards it's return to full strength. Try smelling your favourite flower. If you cannot sense the scent, dub it in. Tell your mind that you can smell it. Remember the smell from the last time you could smell that type of flower.

If you have physical withdrawal symptoms, then you have to stamp your authority on the situation even more heavily. Other people have given up, so why shouldn't you. They got through the pain, so you can too. Just give up and accept nothing less than being a non smoker. Take pleasure in sitting on the no smoking table at work, or in the no smoking compartment of a train. Make the pleasure immense when you reply non smoking, to the girl at the airline check in desk.

You have to make it seem better for you to not

85

smoke, than it is for you to smoke. It is the same with whatever you do. Make what you want attractive, and what you don't want, utterly miserable. See the pleasure in your success, and if you want to contemplate failure at all, make it a dismally miserable experience.

You know, smoking is a problem of our time whether we confront it or not. In a well balanced Advanced PAC Practitioner, I have to say that there is no excuse whatsoever for smoking. You have the technology at your disposal to rid yourself of the damaging habit. I have been through it...I know what I am talking about!

When I began to smoke at school many years ago, had to force myself to like it, but once I had forced myself to smoke a few cigarettes, *they forced me to continue*! My path to ridding myself of the vicious practice began with my eighty year old Grandmother who came to stay with us for a holiday back in 1981. She had smoked for seventy years. One evening, as we were settling into the lounge for a chat, she lit up a cigarette, took a puff from it, and threw it into the coal fire.

"That was my last," she exclaimed.

All it took for her to accomplish this simple task was a decision and a positive purpose. She had no withdrawal symptoms because *she didn't expect any*.

Six months later my Mother gave up the habit after forty years. Then my Mother and Father came to stay with us for a holiday. My Father, who was then sixty eight years old, and had been smoking for

86

almost sixty of those years, without warning stubbed out a cigarette and said, "no more!"

I was embarrassed. What should I do? I was studying the mind and how to improve my mental abilities at the time, and I was encouraging my Family to do the same. Yet they were able to kick a nasty habit at the drop of a hat, and I was still wading in with the old excuse, that I had reached a mental state where I was able to do anything I wanted...and I wanted to smoke.

I wasn't the only one. It was the single most used excuse amongst my peers at the time. We were all travelling the road to mental and spiritual freedom, and so many of us used this same justification.

I did stop however, and the withdrawal symptoms were atrocious! My will power was fierce and I won the fight, even though I put on two stones in weight... *just as* I *had expected*!

There is nothing smoking can provide you with, that isn't available elsewhere. I've heard all the justifications for continuing with the habit...the relaxation excuse... rubbish, the image excuse... garbage. Look, anything that you CAN think of that is pro smoking...is wrong. Get it? So if you haven't given up by now, then just do it and let's move on to richer pastures.

I *enjoy being a non smoker.* I *enjoy being a non smoker.* I *enjoy being a non smoker.* I *have a healthy body*!

I have a little more sympathy for the overeater, but not much. I was two stones overweight before

87

having the good fortune to come across Harvey and Marilyn Diamond's book, *Fit for Life*. It is principally a book about food combining and healthy eating routines. Although it is not strictly speaking a vegetarian publication, I was heavily into vegetarianism and knew every single veggie argument off by heart *with an added twenty percent agents commission on top*.

Boy, when meat eaters saw me on a job, or at a party, you could hear their mental sighs of helplessness

I was a bigot as well. I didn't greet my friends with hello. . .I'd launch straight into a tirade about animal rights and vegetable protein. I could clear a room instantly just by being there. The thing is, I was an excellent talker as well, and I can't remember a single time when someone got the better of me. I thought this was great. . .but they didn't. All I did was alienate my friends by holding on to a viewpoint despite them. The viewpoint took precedence over my friendship with them. I had a good cause, but no one took note because of the bigoted delivery.

I am still vegetarian, as are my Daughter, Eve, Son Luke and Wife, Allison. We felt that our children should ease up on their principled crusade, as they had become more biased and bigoted than ourselves on this issue. I took them to a burger bar and ordered the meatiest burgers available. . .all round. I ate mine and insisted they ate theirs. They wouldn't. . .they just wouldn't. . .and they were disgusted that I did. ate theirs as well. I tried to eat meat for a short time after that but it was a plain fact that I did not like it

I told them all the reasons why they *should* eat meat. . .but the argument was thin and they wouldn't budge on the issue. It wasn't until I had presented them with all the alternative viewpoints, that I felt good about them continuing as vegetarians. They gave me a rough time about it though. Even though I continued as a vegetarian, they derided me as a meat eater for a long time afterwards.

My purpose here is not to espouse the cause or habit of vegetarianism. Merely to point you in the direction of alternative eating customs that you might like to try. You could find the absence of meat from your diet a positive change. You may wish to become a part time veggie. You could consider being a fish only person. . .all I ask of you is to take a look and try.

Get yourself a book from the library on the moral issue. Get another one about the health aspect. At the very least, look at the subject, and if you feel good about it. . .give it a try.

The mistake I made when I became vegetarian, was in thinking that I could eat as much as I liked. I was mistaken. The worst thing you can do is overeat, whether you be vegetarian or meat eater.

Push that plate away when you have had enough. Get into the habit of leaving something on your plate. If you still want to eat for the taste trip, but know that your stomach is full. . .push that plate away and turn up your favourite music. . .loud! Introduce pleasure into the equation. Sing at the top of your voice. . .put your attention onto something else. . .see yourself in the next size down if you are too fat.

I'*m a good weight for my height. I'm a good weight
for my height. I'm a good weight for my height. I'm a
good weight for my height.* **I eat all the right things
and I'm always slim**!

A clever little trick that can work for you is this. Take
chocolate for instance... I used to love chocolate
and consequently ate too much of the stuff. I loved
the taste and the texture. I hated the taste and
texture of lard however. To wean myself of chocolate, I
substituted the mental sensations of lard, for the
ones I associated with chocolate. Eating chocolate
became eating lard, to all intents and purposes
Whenever I ate chocolate... I *thought* lard.

You can do this with anything actually. I call the
trick...

Mental substitution.

It is the art of taking a desirable yet unhealthy
craving, and substituting the mental outlook you have
on that fixation, for an undesirable feeling. Thus
chocolate becomes lard.

Drugs are the menace of our age. I am not an
expert on drugs or medicine, and can tell you only of
limited but interesting experiences.

In 1976, I became a member of an almost drug free
culture. It was a prerequisite of the course for
spiritual enlightenment that I had embarked on, and
I embraced the idea excitedly. I have hardly needed
drugs since the day I agreed to do without them
wherever possible. But let me make one thing quite

clear, if I needed drugs for a sound medical reason, *and I would be the main judge of that,* **then I would take them**.

I am talking about Cough Medicine, Cold Remedies, Headache pills, Pain Killers and other every day drugs. I exclude antibiotics from this list as I do not class them as drugs. There are usually other methods of treating an ailment without resorting to drugs. I have read in various reports, that psycho-somatic illness accounts for up to 90% of the cases that are treated by General Practitioners every day. That means illness induced by the mind... ***self inflicted***!

Voodoo works in a similar way. You get the person to believe that something is going to happen... well, well, well... it happens. The hex, voiced by someone else, is eventually self imposed.

I got out of the habit of relying on Medical Doctors for all but the severest of problems, many years ago. I must also say that I have not had any severe problems since I convinced myself that I had a healthy body. The moment I trusted my inner judgement, and allowed it to take precedence over any other expert opinion, I became my own basic doctor. *This is not a cheap shot at the Medical Profession.* Any Medical Doctor who has studied beyond what was necessary in order for him or her to qualify, will know that there is much more to treating patients than medicine.

My criticism is of you, if you once held, and still hold, the opinion that drugs are a substitute for mental power.

91

Advanced PAC Practitioners hold their own council and judge according to an inner feeling.

I understand that drugs are a useful aid, as much as I understand that they are also a last resort. If I know that the dentist's drill is going to touch a live nerve during treatment, and I also know that I presently have an inability to withstand the resultant pain without jumping and shrieking at the top of my voice, then I also know that it is wise for me to have a pain killing injection in my gum, and I have one.

If there is no nerve in the tooth that is being worked on, then I always request treatment without the painkiller in the first instance... if it hurts, and gets in the way of the treatment... give me the shot.

Society has to end it's fixation on drugs!

It is now time to relegate drugs to the second division.

We must steer our approach to illness in the direction of improving mental power within the patient. *Every course in medicine should begin and end with thorough knowledge of the human mind.*

Drugs for fun? What do you think? Ultimately, as a PAC member, you will shy away from anything over which you do not fully control. I don't take drugs for fun, because I'm bigger than that. *Firstly I made the decision*. My business has a lot less drug involvement than the press would have you believe. Most really successful actors, actresses, singers, musicians and producers, are too busy being successful to involve themselves with drugs.

I often get calls at around 9 in the evening, and I mention to the caller that I was just on my way to bed. It causes amazement. It doesn't seem to tally with the image.

If you have to be on a film set, on a freezing Tuesday morning at the beginning of February, in the London Docklands, at 5am, you can't stay up late the night before, high on LSD, and still look good on camera whilst memorising and delivering your lines. I have worked with many famous people, and they are usually as far removed from their press contrived image as it is possible to conceive.

If drugs are controlling you. . .you aren't!

If you are in the public eye, then you cannot escape your responsibility to the public. You are there because of them. You have a duty to set a good and honourable example. The image of sex, drugs and rock-n-roll doesn't hold true any more. . .if it ever did. Nor does it have to be a kiss on the cheek, Perrier and a little light music. C'mon, you know the scene. PAC People enjoy what is available. . .they know when to start and when to stop. They know when

93

harm is being done. They don't need to ask someone else.

Where would we be without Lucy in the Sky with Diamonds? It's a tricky subject. The imagery created by such a song, I would hate to be without. The so called drug written songs of the sixties were indeed sometimes beautiful, and tugged on emotions little used before in popular music. All I can say is, thank God we have the ideas from this period, and thank God it's in the past. We know what hallucinatory drugs can do, and the things you may be able to see when using them. We know about the feelings and emotions that have been described from such trips. I *also know that anything you can experience with fun drugs, **you can experience safely without***.

I mentioned earlier about copying. That was copying principally to do with money making schemes. Copying can also be done for other reasons. You can copy good examples, copy good behaviour, copy techniques and ***copy exhilarating experiences***. There is even good reason to believe that people with mental disabilities can be encouraged to copy other more fortunate people, and have *the apparency*, in varying degrees, of normality.

It's up to you. Give yourself a challenge. The Phil Potion. The Murray Medicine. The Drug Free Tonic. Try them all. If you are turned on by someone's story of a drug experience...try having that experience without the drug. If I contemplated relying on an artificial stimulant, I would feel smaller. I know that I **am cleverer than that!**

94

Please...when you catch me wearing leather shoes and drinking a pint of Draught Bass, spare me the "alcohol is a drug/animal skin cruelty" arguments, I've heard them all before. I do what I think is right for me at the time.

I recently worked for the BBC, with a Director who was also vegetarian. He was quick to point out that he wore plastic shoes. He said that he was so tired of that old argument that he decided to go the whole way. *Fine*. My decisions are not reliant on what other people think, yet I do remain sensitive to the viewpoint of others.

Be an **Aware PAC Person** and do what you think is right, but don't ever allow yourself the punishment of thinking that ignorance is an excuse. "I didn't know", is just about the worst excuse in the world. "Find out", is possibly the finest antidote.

Drugs are a no-no. You know that...I know that, and now we have to find ways of telling the kids that. We need to increase our emphasis on good fun education...not just academic education, which *is* a big help in itself...we have to get the message across to the kids; in the home, in the playground and on the street. The message is...

I don't need drugs for a real good time

I don't smoke dope and I'm feeling fine

I just love life and I'm high on that

I get turned on with a thought...

Whatever works for you, and whatever works for the kids. Let's head in the right direction...take a bearing on a "Drug Free Culture"!

• • •

95

It is also worth noting whether your prime motivation is towards pleasure, or away from pain. Are you running away from poverty, or towards pleasure. There is nothing wrong with either motivation. The only thing to beware of, is stopping when you have escaped poverty and finding that your motivation has sagged because you are now safe. There is no reason why you cannot have motivation from both areas, and if it isn't there already, then place it there deliberately.

A positive mental attitude, plus good, strong and purposeful action, will equal total success every single time. Do *you hear that*?

A positive attitude, plus a good strong purpose, will equal total success every single time!

Surely that means it is worth spending a bit of time on your attitude and checking your purpose. If your purpose, or reason for doing something, is strong enough, it will always make you win. Don't ever forget that *determination is the common denominator with all success*. *You have to keep on keeping on*.

You can always get what you want... *if you are determined to get it*!

I find *that*, the most exciting feeling in the world. To know that I can have whatever I want, without compromising my reality of honesty and integrity, is absolutely exhilarating! You can get excited about those things too. Positively charge your desires with as much excitement as possible, know who is in charge, and demand what you want from life.

Have FAITH in your own success and don't ever doubt yourself. Have FAITH in the SM. Have FAITH in **Premier Imagination**. Have **FAITH** in your goal.

FAITH is an important part of the formula.

FAITH is a vital ingredient. When you set a goal you must have total FAITH in your ability to accomplish that task. Make the SM work for you, and have FAITH that it will succeed.

A light thought, can have more desire, FAITH and emotion in it, than a heavy, laboured one.

The SM will accept a command no matter how light or whispy it may be. Passing thoughts and transient desires will often amaze you when they happen. What I am teaching you, is how to control yourself for personal success, and that includes programming yourself, so that passing thoughts and transient desires become *part* of the success process.

Eventually, every single thought that passes through your mind will be positive. That means you could decide to be in Australia for Christmas, and Brazil for the same Christmas. The two desires would fight themselves, and this is where single mindedness comes into the equation.

Your positive attitude must be mixed with a *gentle and giving* single mindedness.

Definiteness, but not ruthlessness!

You cannot allow yourself to be blown off course. How many people have given up, with land in sight? Your success could be just around the corner, and it is that *SANE single mindedness* that will make you turn the corner to get what you have been striving for.

You must also accept success as it is presented to you. Was Columbus a failure because he didn't discover *exactly* what he was looking for? There are many ways to interpret success, and it is important that at no time do you punish yourself with an inability to accept success, or portions of it, as and when it comes your way.

Life will pay whatever price you ask of it!

If there is something you don't like about your life...change it. Demand to be in control of your head. Use your brain as a servant. Control it, as you would command a computer.

You have urges in many different directions, and many varying aspects to your life. Can you imagine how you could accelerate your progress to success if these aspects and directions were all channelled to the same course. Naturally this is not totally possible. You have to eat, you have to see the family, fix the gutters, check the oil, and so on and on...

You can however, *take specific energy that is being misused, or under used, and make it help you succeed*. The *sex urge* is an important part of your existence. It is fun, it is vital to the continuation of the species, it is part of you...YOU may be identified with *your* particular urge.

The truth is, that sex is only really needed for procreation. Most of us have, on average, two children. We probably need to have sex less than 20 times in our lives for it to have fulfilled it's purpose.

You can channel this power into your drive for success.

Ultimately, you can transfer this urge for sex, and all it's ramifications and complications, into your assault on success. Your partner would have to understand! Your partner would have to be in agreement! I am talking essentially to those of you who have completed your family, but the principle stands in varying degrees, for every person on the Planet.

Success is SEXY!

The sex urge is tangible and readily understood by most of us. You can see that it is an incredibly powerful driving force. It makes you get things done. It pushes you past the post, when you would have given up had the object not been sex. It makes you aware of yourself. It gives you a magnetism to others. This urge makes you attractive. It is a reason for great accomplishment.

This book is not about sex. I tell you this data, because it works. Transmutation of the sex urge is possible. I give you the option, and leave the choice of whether or not to use this device, entirely up to you.

• • •

There have been massive leaps forward recently in our knowledge of the brain, most especially it's potential and capabilities. But most significantly, how to get into it the knowledge you wish to remember. The results of research into left and right brain activity, and how we can use both brains to full advantage, is so helpful.

There is a book called *Accelerated Learning* by Colin Rose, and an organisation of the same name, which specialises in technology fundamentally connected to education, but having far more uses than may at first be apparent. Whatever works for you in education, can also work for you in any mental situation where you need to feed information into your Sub Conscious Mind.

Richard Bandler and John Grinder, established the importance of the three different ways to communicate with Human Beings. This became the basis of Neuro Linguistic Programming.

Visual, Auditory and Kinaesthetic.

The latter simply means to do with movement or action.

This discovery seems obvious doesn't it...but let's look at the implications. There is no point in trying to teach a visual oriented person with an audio tape, because it won't work as well as a video, or live show. Action oriented people would find data absorption easier if they were allowed to act it out.

You have to inject data into yourself by the method that you find acceptable. SEE, hEAR or ACTion.

You can often tell what system people use most, by the way they communicate...phrases like..."I see what you mean", or, "I get the picture", can indicate a visual person. "I hear what you are saying", or, "that sounds stupid to me", should tell you that this person leans towards the auditory. "Feels good to me", or, "give me a solid example", shows a kinaesthetic approach to life.

Okay, this new data can be used in sales. When you are selling a car to an auditory person, don't keep talking about how the car looks...you would say things like..."listen to the hi fi, doesn't that sound beautiful?" Or, "let's take a ride and hear how she sounds."

I am more interested in getting you to use this data in programming yourself for total success. Find out what your leaning is, and use it to full advantage, *just as a salesman would use it on you.*

If you are a visual person, *see* your goals as already accomplished. If you are auditory, *hear* the accomplishment. Listen to what people are saying about you…"didn't he do well"…"I heard that it's the biggest selling record of all time." If you are primarily kinaesthetic, then feel the ride of the car, hold on to that feeling of success, and give yourself a solid feeling of accomplishment.

Another valuable technique available to you is called anchoring.

In education for instance, if you were *to remember* a time when you learnt something new and felt good about it, like swimming, or riding a bike for instance, you would show the same physiological reactions as you did when you first experienced the learning for real. If you then touch your wrist or your shoulder, at the same time as remembering that experience, this will become *an anchor*.

In future, just by using the anchor…touching the shoulder or the wrist…you will be able to tap into the same enthusiasm and success that you initially felt. I call this…

Tuning in to the WIN!

If I am just about to take part in an important meeting, I firstly visualise the desired finished outcome as already happened, and I then *tune in to a win* of a similar type from my past.

In 1979, I had a major recording contract with one of the most successful labels in Britain. They let it be known that they were about to drop me. My manager and I parted company, and I felt demoralised and dejected. . .for a few minutes.

I decided that I would try someone else's song in an effort to refresh my involvement with the company. I remembered a massive hit from the previous year. I discovered who had written it. I remembered that person as having recorded at the same London studio that I used for an album in 1976/1977. I called the studio up and got the telephone number of the partner of this person. I used the power of the record company to make it sound worth his while to get a song to me, written by his partner. Before this song was forthcoming, I set a meeting up with the boss of the record company and the two partners.

The meeting occurred and I wasn't even mentioned.

The partners instead, were offered a £100,000 contract to produce one of the company's top groups. They turned the offer down for various reasons.

I pleaded for the song anyway, and it was given to me. I realised that the boss of the company I was with, was into getting successful producers and songwriters involved with him. I *would give him both*. I took a cassette demo of the song up to the St John's Wood offices and studios, and decided to somehow reopen dialogue with him on the subject of *Phil Murray*.

He was in the studio mixing a new recording with one of his other groups. I waited outside that studio door without moving for more than three hours. I wanted to eat, wanted to drink, wanted the bathroom...but I fixed my attention on him, and was totally single minded about the outcome of our meeting...which he didn't even know was going to occur.

At last he came out of the door...

"I've got a hit song here, written by a hit songwriter, and produced by hit producers who I know you want to use...can I have three minutes of your time?" I asked.

He led me into his office and listened to the cassette. I could see that he was excited. He said that I could record the song anywhere in the world using any musicians I wished. He walked me through the record company telling all the staff, who previously hadn't been returning my telephone calls, to give me whatever I needed to help with the recording... **I was walking on air and living my dream**. I quickly called the producers...who hadn't exactly agreed to produce me, and got their agreement.

We recorded the song, and although it wasn't a massive hit in it's own right, because of a change in distribution companies midway through it's heaviest span of airplay, it found it's way onto a compilation album which sold in excess of 250,000 copies.

I *tune in to this scene whenever* I *am trying to get something done*. **I remember this success**. I remember the feeling, when I was told that I could record the song anywhere in the world. You will have time periods in your life which can be a source of deep inspiration to you now. Find them!

Tune in to SUCCESS, and remember the power of the SM!

People were appalled when they discovered that a cinema in the United States, had flashed subliminal messages onto the screen, encouraging the audience to buy products available in the foyer. Their sales increased by up to 50%. The audience couldn't see the messages because the flashes were too quick. The Sub Conscious Mind saw them though, and caused the people to act according to what it had been told was good.

Use your Subconscious Mind...it does as it is told.

Be definite, do not get waylaid, and remember that determination is the common denominator of all success.

If you need to rid yourself of unwanted feelings in uncomfortable incidents housed in your memory, then you need to use the **ZIP *formula***. I include this tip in my book as it will help those of you who are hung up on incidents from the past.

This is so simple.

Find the picture, incident or memory, that is bothering you, and look at it from beginning to end. When you reach the end, ZIP through it backwards quickly, in just a few seconds. You'll get it. *Zip through it backwards in just a few seconds*. This will wipe out the uncomfortable concepts from the

105

memory, and the picture *without* the unwanted emotion will remain. This works! It puts you in control of your memories. The SM *can* understand this fast ZIP backwards. The SM works at a remarkable speed.

Zipping is simple.

I also utilise a technique which I call. . .

Pinpointing.

I first used this trick when I began performing in large venues. Up until 1976, I had mainly played small clubs, where the audience were continually visible. Suddenly I was singing in a band, who were playing City Halls and Ballrooms. It was a big step up, and I found myself performing to the first few rows of the audience only, and alienating those people that I couldn't see, because of the lights shining in my eyes.

After trying various cures for this common performance deficiency, I discovered my ability to P*inpoint*.

This involved a mental orientation for myself within the venue. I would P*inpoint* the corners of the Auditorium in front of me, and when I had located them mentally, I would perform the same exercise for the corners behind me. It seemed that once I had performed the Pinpointing operation, my communications would travel as far as my Pinpoints. **I *could project as far as* I *could see . . . mentally*.**

I perfected this trick during a six week European

106

Tour of gigantic venues, which included sports arenas and huge municipal complexes. That was in 1977, and we ended the tour by playing the Reading Festival.

We were backstage right up until it was our time to play. When we hit the stage, I saw thirty thousand people stretching farther than the eye could see. I began my Pinpointing process, but it was in the open air, and I had no corners to pinpoint, as had become my habit. Before I could find a solution to this problem, we began the first number. Well, just about everything you could imagine went wrong in that first song.

Perhaps we all had the same Pinpointing problem...the song was out of time...we stopped after the instrumental introduction and tried to regain the correct tempo...none of the band could hear properly...I pulled the microphone from it's stand and the lead came out. When the microphone was fixed, my knees began to knock together...literally. This had never, and hasn't ever since, happened to me.

We had played the first five songs of our set, before I was able to get a bearing on the extremity of the audience, who by this time were thoroughly disinterested. We didn't ever discuss that performance, as I believe we were so completely embarrassed by the experience.

I use Pinpointing in meetings. It helps me orientate myself within a room. It stabilises me in an unusual environment, and makes me feel strong in uncommon surroundings. It is invaluable when speaking in public!

Pinpointing is a trick which *you* can utilise.

• • •

So now is the time to remind yourself who is in charge, and check your blueprint for success. Get healthy, rid yourself of bad, unwanted habits, tune in to success, determination and definiteness...and make sure that you have at least one...

principle centred, long term goal...

stage six

principle centred, long term goals

> ...total success is the continuing involvement in the pursuit of a worthy ideal, which is being realised for the benefits of others—rather than at their expense...
> *Dennis Waitley*

There is no mystery about goal setting. A goal is not something that has a divine comportment. A goal does not have to have a spiritual presence in the **ETHER WAVES** before it descends on you and takes over your being. Goals do not usually seek you out.

You have to make up your own goals!

You have to take responsibility from the very beginning, you see. Through the ages, we have heard stories of great men and women who spoke of being given their goal in life by a "Higher Being". I don't deny that this is possible. What I am saying to you is this...don't sit around waiting for the call.

There is no excuse for no goals!

A goal can be small or medium size, long term or short term, huge, divine, spiritual, worldly, small minded or even someone else's. Anything can be a goal. I know something else for sure. Every single person reading this has set at least one goal for themselves. You bought this book and you are reading it. . . or maybe you just borrowed it because you didn't *set the goal of owning it for yourself.*

Reading a book on success is a waste of time if you do not *practice* your new found knowledge. I was looking through the Psychology/Inspirational/Motivational section of a major bookstore, when a lady said to me that someone should write a book on "How To Wean Yourself Off Motivational Books", and I very nearly did! Many people get high on the success stories of others, and do not administer the principles that produced this success, into their own lives.

It is an easy mistake!

I know that people view a lot of their education as a waste of time because "they have no intention of using it in their lives". Everything that you learn has a bearing on your future. . . treasure each piece of knowledge and use it fully.

A favourite viewpoint at my school was that learning Latin was a waste of time. German, French and Spanish were far more useful. Dead languages should be avoided, and the Latin class had only three pupils.

I subsequently discovered that Latin was alive and well in just about every aspect of the English language. I cannot think of anything that would have been more helpful to me in writing, than a good grounding in Latin.

You may not be aware of yourself using knowledge. Your *successful use of knowledge* may not at first be apparent to you. But you can bet your life that you are demonstrating in your every day life exactly what you have studied and believed.

If you read garbage newspapers that espouse bigoted viewpoints, then you have to expect your intake to reflect into your life. If your friends are negative, and you are frequently in contact with them, their negativity will scrape away at your positivity. If the people around you have low expectations of life . . . if your environment is down tone . . . if your dress is sloppy . . . if your body is unwashed . . . if your job is depressing . . . if your spouse is antagonistic . . .

It is your duty as an Advanced PAC Member, to surround yourself with inspiration and beauty. Quality and craftsmanship. Classic and mighty aesthetic appeal . . . poetry and lyric. Music and the sound of silence. TTM and TFT. Knowledge of the SM and CM. *Premier Imagination and Secondary Imagination*.

Surround yourself with great ideas!

Check your Supergroup for positive charge, *and eliminate any negative charge*. Give your Family the once over, and help them stay on the bright side.

Never ever-ever compromise with what is real to you!

You've all set goals. Deciding to eat in a certain

restaurant someday is setting a goal. Deciding on the size of your Family is goal setting.

Do you realise the power of goal setting?

Can you imagine how damaging it would be for you to set the wrong goal for yourself? We need to look at this subject carefully so that we may use this powerful goal technology to it's fullest.

First of all, I am taking for granted the fact that you...whoever you are, or whatever you think you are...are a cut above the rest. *Any person who contemplates improvement for any aspect of their life, is moving on up the ladder*. I want you to thoroughly acknowledge yourself for taking steps towards your own personal success. Pat yourself on the back...congratulate yourself...welcome yourself to the *real* big time...I mean it...do those things. Talk to yourself now, and get excited about the future.

Write fifty lines that say, I *thank myself for my success*!

I have read various reports that seem to put anyone who has a goal, and a plan for the accomplishment of that goal, into the top 2% of the population who are likely to achieve personal success.

Forget about the past...it's gone and will never return. *Develop a nostalgia for the future*. An excitement about just what is in store for you. Can you believe that just by mapping out your life right now, and saying what you intend to accomplish with your plan, you put yourself into that top 2%.

Can you afford not to map out your life?

A ship without a course! An explorer without a compass. A city without a map. What are you . . . a piece of driftwood . . . or a powerful speed boat heading for a port in Paradise? *The choice is yours*!

There are leaders and followers. Neither one is necessarily better than the other. Your goal can be connected to either. It seems that followers can expect less financial reward than their leaders, but I cannot see how we could have leaders without anyone to lead. Decide if your goal is in leadership or not, and be happy about falling into either category.

Get a piece of paper and a pen and write down the one thing that you intend to do with your life, without reference to anything else whatsoever, *apart from you*. Care nothing for what other people may think. Don't feel that you are "*too big for your boots*" if you set too high a target. This exercise will cost you nothing, and give you a massive boost.

If the Genie agreed to grant you one wish to do with your life, what would you ask for?

Write down your answer.

If you have an answer written down on paper . . . that's fine. If you don't have that one answer . . . fine

113

also. Not everyone has just one thing that they want to do with their lives, or one magnificent obsession! At the very least I want you to write down *a few things* that you would like to do with your life.

If you do not have that one burning ambition, then write down whatever it is you would rather do, than something else.

If you have anything written down on that paper, then you should feel good about yourself. I predict that you are on the way to personal success.

Next you need a plan for the accomplishment of your goal. A step by step guide to your own fulfilment. Who do you need to meet? What information do you need? What, where, who and how?

My goals have been with songs and singing ever since I was seven. I remember planning a musical just before I went to sleep one night. I shouted to my Mother and told her all about it. That idea came complete with staging plans and performers. I moved on to a tape recorder and made up my own programmes. My imagination worked for me.

When I was sixteen, I helped form a band, and began writing my first songs in earnest. In 1972 I remember being asked in a local magazine interview, what my ambition was. I said that it was to record at Trident Studios in London. Lots of music that I admired had been recorded there, and it was an extremely successful studio.

In 1973, I remember going to see David Bowie at Newcastle City Hall. Before Bowie hit the stage, the Spiders from Mars appeared. The drummer sat at the kit holding a stick on each of his tom toms and stared straight at the audience. The Spiders looked terrific. I turned to my then Girlfriend and now Wife, and told her that someday I would play with those musicians . . . especially the drummer.

They were the top band in the world at the time, and I was the singer in a local group, mainly playing social clubs, and using other peoples' songs. In 1975, my guitarist and friend, called me excitedly and asked me to visit him for a chat. He had recorded an album with his other band, which had not sold well, but had been heard by the Spiders from Mars . . . they were looking for a new guitarist and had asked him to join. What should he do? He asked me, because if he left us, his leaving would put my band in the awkward position of having to find a replacement as good as him, at short notice.

I told him to join as quickly as possible, which he did. They recorded an album and toured, but went the way of most groups and split in 1976. I was living in London by that time, and had returned to the North East for a weekend. I bumped into my friend as soon as I arrived, and he asked if the drummer from the Spiders had called me, as he was looking for a singer to form a new band with.

I remembered my goal and got that excited feeling in my stomach. He hadn't called so I called him. That night, I travelled back down south to

London, then onwards to East Grinstead the next morning. The drummer and I talked, we played, formed the band, and made our first recordings at. . . guess where? Trident Studios, London. We then toured and recorded an album. We became the best of friends. We then got a tour supporting a big name band, who were looking for a bass player. The job went to the original Spiders bass player. We then toured together for six weeks.

When we returned to East Grinstead, the original Spiders guitarist visited. We were playing in London the following night and the bass player and guitarist were coming to the gig. All three of them in one place. . .guess what happened? No we didn't play together!

That goal had become a kind of *self fulfilling prophecy* with energy of it's own. When the time came for it to reach it's conclusion, my interest had diminished. My new goals for writing and performing successful songs had taking over. It was however, of more than a passing interest to me, when I saw just how far that goal ran, and seemingly of it's own accord.

You can change your goal.

The goal isn't sacred. The goal is a tool. Use it for your own selfish aims. Use it for the betterment of the world. Use it to give or to get. But whatever you do, use it! **This goal technology works**. . . other people are using it, and getting *amazing results*, so why don't you?

I want to talk to you about happiness. I have asked

116

many people about their goals, and happiness always seems to be in there somewhere. Often it is the main goal, and a fine idea at that.

The problem with happiness, is that it seems to come along as a by-product on the way to somewhere else. If you are looking for happiness itself, then what exactly is it? Where is it?

Happiness comes while you are doing something else.

It seems that it is not an end point in itself. Rather, you become happy when you are doing whatever it is that you feel you want to do. When you are doing something you don't want to do then it seems that unhappiness comes along. You can't do happiness... you have to do something else and accept happiness as a by-product.

If you want money from a goal then it must have some kind of service built into it. If your goal is to travel...I can't see money forthcoming, unless you qualify the travel with some kind of service. Writing for instance. Courier work. War corespondent.

Choose your goals wisely.

They can be with you for a long time, as my previous example has proved. If you haven't honed the finer points, and the goal has rough edges, then be prepared for exactly what you have planned, to arrive on your doorstep. Your Sub Conscious Mind

YOU CAN ALWAYS GET WHAT YOU WANT

will strive to deliver exactly what you told it you wanted!

We moved to America for a time, and then back to our native North East of England for a couple of years. We worked so hard that we really felt as though we were becoming a little too divorced from our spiritual leanings, than we cared to admit. We decided to move back to the East Grinstead area where I had lived since 1976, and bought a house in Felbridge, Surrey. All the time we were living away from this area, and whenever we had difficulties in business, we used to say to each other, what would our friend Jay do in this situation? This eased our attention from immediate difficulties, but also allowed us to use his viewpoint. . . or his viewpoint as we interpreted it. We took someone else on board at no extra cost.

Just before we made the move back down south, we felt that this guy Jay was just the person to get our business back on the tracks. He would have the answers. Jay would get the ball rolling.

We had looked after his daughter when my wife and I first lived together in the late seventies, and he had been the Minister who married us in 1980.

It was Jay who I bumped into at the new year party plus one in 1993. It was Jay who reminded me of goals and targets, and Jay who introduced me to a whole host of new and very positive goodies.

The business took on a new momentum!

I thought that if this friend of mine could inspire me that far, then there was more to be had. He introduced me to a Brian Tracy programme called the

Psychology of Success. I then borrowed the Anthony Robbins book Ultimate Power, from him. I later bought it, and everything else that I could lay my hands on to do with getting what you want from life. He introduced me to Maxwell Maltz's Psycho-Cybernetics, Accelerated Learning and Neuro Linguistic Programming. I read Dale Carnegie's, *How to Win Friends and Influence People*.

Meanwhile I was working, and my business was gaining more momentum. I went to Jay's American Independence Day party, and he told me about Napoleon Hill. I found myself a copy of *Think and Grow Rich*. From these beginnings I went on to discover Steven Covey, Shad Helmstetter, Dennis Waitley and Wayne Dyer. There are many people out there, discovering and writing about powerful technology to do with improving the lot of the Human Being. And of course there are still the powerful teachings from the old religions.

The point of me telling you all this. . . we expected Jay to help us, and we had half a plan for getting him interested in the music business. The help we expected came from him, and we were quick to realise it had taken on a form other than what had been expected. We had got exactly what we had decided we would get. We took all that came with open arms and heaps of gratitude.

Look out for the curve!

You may have planned and worked hard, expecting

119

a return from a certain place and in a certain way. Your dreams will be answered, but it may not be as obvious as you would expect. Be determined and flexible. There are many paradoxes in the field of human behavioural improvement. There are those who believe in a Supreme Being who has everything mapped out for you, but that you still have self determination and the ability to change events. You must decide for yourself on the subject of paradoxes.

Paradoxical situations always run the risk of ridiculing any subject, most of all a subject as sensitive as The Human Being. If you predict success for yourself in a given field, with massive amounts of money as a by-product of your service, you have to accept that the financial reward could come from anywhere. You could win the Premium Bonds, or the Pools!

I must also say, that while we are talking about personal success, earning loads of money, and extracting from life exactly what we want from it . . . it is worth noting that no matter how you approach life, there is nothing greater than the ability of being able to give to others.

It is impossible to be a great giver and also unsuccessful in life!

How do you like that one? It is an immutable law of the universe, which states that, what you give you get. When you give, you create a vacuum. That vacuum has to be filled. What you put out, you have to get back.

Plant good seed...what you harvest will reflect exactly what you have sown!

There is no reason at all why any goal cannot contain honesty, integrity and winning for all. In any situation, no matter what it is, there is a formula in there somewhere allowing all parties to win. If your goal contains the win for all ingredient then you have the force of good on your side. I am not saying that you cannot win without someone else winning. There is a shallow win formula, and a deep win formula. You have the choice of paths.

A Mission Statement will help you.

When you write out on paper exactly what your mission in life is, then it will tell you a lot about yourself. A Personal Mission Statement (or PMS) is a valuable document. Every true Advanced PAC Member has a Mission Statement for him or herself, his or her business (a BMS) and his or her Family (an FMS). That is a minimum of three Mission Statements.

If you have not already compiled your three Mission Statements, then now is the time to do it.

Your PMS should be exactly that. Personal. To do with *you*. What you are going to do in life. The influence you aim to have on society. Everything to do with *you*.

I share my PMS with you in the hope that it will be inspirational and set you a good example.

PHIL MURRAY
MISSION STATEMENT

1
I write quality songs, plays, novels, articles,
Success Literature and Inspirational
Material

2
I record quality songs and
Inspirational Material

3
I research and write Success
Formulas and Goal Techniques

4
I am an excellent live performer

5
I have an expanding public who buy
my products

6
I expand PWM as a business vehicle
for myself and others

7
I have recognition within the
entertainment and motivational industries

8
I am the biggest selling
writer/singer/songwriter/producer, ever

9
I am known as an artiste of quality and integrity

10
I am a good actor

11
I write stories and plays that people enjoy

12
I am a successful person

13
I am a strong Family man

14
I am a good Husband and Father

15
I enjoy life to it's full

I am wealthy
I am successful
I earn in excess of £100,000 per year
I earn this money from many enjoyable sources
People like my work
I am popular
I am good at my job
I am a good Father
I am a good husband
I always have time for my Family

I always have time for my Friends
I have a second home in Florida
I own two new cars
I give lots to charity
I always keep 10% of my income
My income is always increasing
I adore being rich
Being rich allows me to be more spiritual
I am constantly improving myself
spiritually
I like myself
I like myself
I like myself

•　　•　　•

Your BMS is a statement of intention to do with your business. I know of businesses that have at the base of their modus operandi, the desire to increase the asset base of the owners. Well, a BMS is a little more complicated than a PMS... because it has more involvement with other people.

A narrow minded Admiral is more likely to incite mutiny than a caring Captain. How to avoid a rough passage...

You may well own the business on paper, but to the degree that other people are helping with it's success, then they have a stake also. Employees and their families, suppliers, retailers, wholesalers, and the public. All of these people have to be included in the aims and aspirations of *any* business! You have to include them *all* in your BMS. If you wish to avoid the. . . I just do as I'm told, attitude, more than my job's worth, it's not worth my while, that isn't my job, you've got the wrong department, sorry I can't help, and I don't know who can! . . . then get your BMS honed finely. Show everyone that you care. . . then care some more! Everyone connected with your business has to win!

When I work in Studios on projects that are dear to my heart, and I see that there is a youngster on work experience in the building, I always invite them in while I am working. I think of how I would have felt at their age to be in their situation, and I share as much of my knowledge with them as I think it is fair to expect them to assimilate. The Studio may not belong to me. These people are not on work experience with me. But they are part of my BMS.

If they will accept. . . then I will give.

If your BMS is honourable, then without a shadow of a doubt, that fact alone at the base of your modus operandi, will place your business above others with less honourable aims.

Think of everyone connected with your business, and compose your Business Mission Statement around them.

I share with you the Mission Statement for my company.

PeRFECT WORDS and MUSIC
MISSION STATEMENT

1
We honestly and successfully market
quality works and artistes, worldwide

2
We provide a secure and enjoyable
working environment for all employees

3
We always see things long term

4
We never ever take short cuts
to the detriment of a product

5
We are seen as an honest and
successful company within
our industry

6
We are involved in every aspect of
the entertainment and motivational
business

7
We are innovative and cherish
our relationships within the company

8
We are helpful to others within the
business

9
We are wealthy market leaders

10
We maintain dignity at all times

• • •

An FMS must likewise reflect the needs and aspirations of your complete family. For that reason alone, it will need to be a group composition. Harmonious and successful living will be achieved far more quickly and easily, with an aligned Family Mission Statement, that has been written by the whole family.

This is our FMS.

THE MURRAY FAMILY
MISSION STATEMENT

1
We love each other as best friends

2
We listen to each other with interest

3
We are kind to one another

4
We always have time for each other

5
We have fun

6
We learn from each other

7
We live in a creative environment

8
We are creative as a Family

9
We play together

10
We achieve a high level of education

11
We travel the world

12
We experience new things together

13
We are successful as a Family

14
We are wealthier every day in every way

15
We are the best Family in the world

• • •

You may also want an Extended Supergroup Mission Statement. Talk to the other members and get their agreement. I am convinced that it will inspire you all, and for the short time that it will take to compose, it will pay you back a thousand fold.

This technology that I am discovering and passing on to you, is the very heart of life itself. It will produce very strong individuals . . . but the strongest of you all will be those that learn the art of interdependence.

You can be independent and interdependent without hypocrisy.

Interdependence has giving to others at it's source point. It is not the *art of taking*, but the *skill of giving* to others, and accepting a return when it comes. If you have set up a business that involves inter departmental rivalry, can you honestly sit down and tell me, especially after reading this book, that this rivalry is a healthy option to mutually co-operative methods. Where there is rivalry, there is duplicity. Where there is duplicity, there is a down tone environment. Where this attitude prevails, true achievers do not go.

True achievers have peace of mind as a fulcrum. They balance themselves, and if they feel at any time that they have dropped beneath the sight of their horizons, they will depart for healthier pastures. Part of their success formula includes inner happiness. *Achievement in the physical world is part of that, **but not the greater part***.

If you want success, then it is wise to have successful people around you. For this to happen, you have to create a desirable environment. If it is duplicitous, then you will attract people who enjoy that atmosphere. What I am saying is that those people will not be the most conducive to your own success.

You need to create a true interdependent situation with a happy atmosphere. Good cycles of communication have to be adopted as the norm. You have to be able to give colleagues your time. There is little that can make a fellow feel worse, than for him to sense that you don't have that time.

This data is valuable for any aspect of life.

When you have listened to someone, let them know that you are interested in their communication, by asking a question about what has just been said. *Ask about a certain aspect of a particular point*. This will also help you to become a true listener. Leave a respectful communication gap, before delivering your response. Ensure that your reply illustrates your complete understanding of what has just been said. Do not interrupt!

You will be astounded by the effect this has on the

people around you. In his time, Dale Carnegie was reputed to have been an incredible *conversationalist*, because of his ability to sit and *listen* with *interest*. This is an important practice to add to your list of attributes as an Advanced PAC Practitioner.

Using a person's name is a powerful tool. People like to be known by their name. It is a "BUTTON" of our time to be thought of as a number. You can show how important a person is to you by using their name. Physical contact can also establish good rapport. A warm handshake and a "hello. . .first name" where appropriate, is obvious. . . but so many people don't do it.

Advanced PAC Practitioners make it their business to know the finer details of a colleague's likes and dislikes. When you remember the birthday of the daughter of an employee, and you send her a card, can you imagine the impact this one small action has on this person's life? CAN you SEE how this will HELP *you*?

How often do you COMPLIMENT the people around you? Can you see the value of a COMPLIMENT? Now I am not suggesting for one moment that your new life has to be filled with flattery, lies and cheap tricks. I guarantee you this. . .you need never lie when giving COMPLIMENTS. Find out what you like about someone and focus on that point. Every living person has some good quality about them. As you become well versed in the ways of POSITIVITY, then so will focusing on the good become more automatic. Always COMPLIMENT the truth!

If you have employees who continually "get it wrong", there will always be something that they do WELL. Continue to COMPLIMENT those points that they do WELL. Those people will do everything in their power to get all the minus points up to the quality of their good points...because you have given them MOTIVATION.

People like to please people.

You are surrounded by ALLIES. Always present them with reasons to like you even more. GENUINE-ness will be natural to PAC Practitioners who have truly cognited on this condition of POSITIVITY that they must aspire towards *on a continual basis*. Your communication skills are a direct reflection of your state of BEING.

You cannot deliver a tirade to your workforce and expect them to feel good about you. You can't show temper and preach peace. You dare not be seen as duplicitous whilst advocating the theories and practices of my book. People in glass houses should not throw stones. Exude the right formula and expect good results. "You get what you give", yet the modern slant to that old phrase is, "give as good as you get".

No-no-no! If you aren't satisfied with what you get, give some more. PAC people do not depend on "the weather" for their moods.

ADVANCED PAC PRACTITIONERS MAKE THEIR OWN WEATHER!

You are the Creator. You are the Source Point. You are Numero Uno... top of the class, head of the queue, leading the league, first in the table... To be those things you have to MAKE YOUR OWN WEATHER!

That translates into every day life like this... no one can ever make you what you don't want to be. Your mood is not dependant on external stimuli. Your quality of communication is not based on the incoming calibre of confabulation. You are a PAC Member, and these points are essential ingredients of Advanced Practice. You have two ears, and one mouth... that should help you remember what ratio of listening to talking you should aim for.

I attended a very good Grammar School where it was cool to be rebellious. Two ingredients of that insurrection were smoking and foul language. In the subject of the latter I excelled. I was able to cut a swot down to size at twenty paces. I carved a niche for myself as head of the school of new language. We only spoke in obscenities, and anyone using inoffensive language was immediately punished for being obsequious.

One of the basic tenets of my new school was that this new language *had to be used*. Once we had devised a new vulgar profanity, it would then have to be employed immediately, preferably on someone to whom it would cause maximum offence.

When this offence was apparent, I would then get the victims to place their hands covering their mouths, and get them to say this latest blasphemous creation that had upset them. If they were soft enough

to do this, I would say . . . "See, words don't hurt do
they!"

Words can hurt!

Words are designed to convey a meaning, and of
course they can hurt. You must choose your words
wisely, and always remember that the Sub Conscious
Mind translates words literally . . . not poetically,
lyrically, beautifully, or metaphorically . . . LITERALLY.

The Sub Conscious Mind translates words literally.

Confession is powerful therapy and involves being
listened to. As the ability to listen increases, then the
skill of hearing exactly what is being said grows.

This means duplicating communication as it is intended, and not as interpreted.

The game of Chinese Whispers is not so unreal as
you may imagine. It involves a circle of people . . . the
first person whispers something like . . . "I know a
game where everyone wins and the game is simply
life". By the time it reaches the last person it has
become . . . "It's just not the same and I love to sin
and I don't mean with my wife".

Communication breakdowns can be repaired by
resuming communication. Stalemate is the worst
situation. Not speaking. No dialogue. Lips sealed.

You begin to rely on the third party.

The power of the third party is wicked!

There is you and the other person, and a third person. When you hear from a third party that someone has said something about you that is derogatory, the power of that disparaging communication is multiplied forcefully. It follows that if your best friend recommends a Phil Murray album to you, then chances are higher of you both getting a copy, and enjoying it. The third party can interfere with good judgement. *Keep your communication lines clean*.

Don't listen to gossip. Gossip is another word for garbage. Demand good sources of information. Exact rumour free dialogue from your colleagues.

Do not speak disparagingly of even your worst enemy.

Work at making your enemies good friends, but meanwhile, don't let anyone know of any disagreements you have with anyone, and never expect a third party to repair a relationship for you. Meet these situations head on, and confront your new life for yourself. Remember that others are listening to you, and most people understand the simple principle that if you speak about someone else in a certain way, then chances are you will speak about *them* in the same way. Don't say unkind things about ANYONE.

A mediator is a powerful person. If there is ever a time in your life when you feel there is no alternative to such a person, then choose wisely.

Beware of rumour mongers!

The act of communicating in parallels and parables can make an otherwise unpalatable communication tolerable. If you need to chastise someone, then you would be wise to show by example in others, where they went wrong. Let them cognite for themselves what happened. Let them tell *you*.

You can't ever gain altitude or respect by demanding it. These two honours are awarded to you by others, and your methods of communication will go a long way towards these awards coming sooner, rather than later, or worse still not at all.

• • •

You can live a life of quick fixes. Lots of short term wins, and plenty of activity. But for ultimate success, as well as quick fixes, you have to have long term goals which have an intrinsic ingredient of good principles. When all the quick fixes are over, you will still be there. When all the fast friends have departed for so called faster more exciting quick fixes, unless you are with them, you will still have to deal with yourself.

You have to have a blueprint. You have to have a plan. You have to work towards the fulfilment of a goal. You have to have a purpose for living.

I often ask people in my profession about their goals. The most prevalent reply that I get is, "I *just want to be famous*"! I call this the "*malaiseyness*" symptom of our age. The striving for fame! Fame has become the end product. . .and yet fame is not *really* an accomplishment. The playing of the piano is the achievement. Fame is the by-product. The writing of the song is the feat. Fame is the consequence.

Too many people want to be famous.

We applaud fame and ignore talent.

We have meteorologists starring in theatrical productions. *The Weather Girl puts bottoms on seats*!

The Radio One Disc Jockey is more bookable than the graduate of stage school.

The book written by the wife of a serial killer, is more desirable than the one that has just won the Booker Prize.

A page three girl from a newspaper can sell out a number one tour. . .but the local band who write and rehearse every day of their lives because that is their *purpose*, cannot get coverage in their town news-paper.

We have to see the aspiration for talent as an applaudable strength. We must encourage the gathering of skill. We should reward the ambition of achievement. We *can* subsidise the weak in their struggle for genuine competence.

Skill, adeptness, deftness, dexterity, mastery, proficiency, ability, capacity, talent, faculty and craft.

Murderers are famous. Anyone can become famous! Don't JUST strive for FAME!

You choose your goals. Why not choose big goals. Why not choose honesty and integrity. Give yourself the challenge of finding *the win for all ingredient*. There can be no true success unless everyone involved with that success has won.

The win for all ingredient is magic.

You can have "you win and they lose" . . . "you lose and they win" . . . "you lose and they lose" . . . or "*you win and they win*".

Find the win for all ingredient and you will have total success. In a deal, all parties will be happy. You will be able to do business again, because you took the time to find the win for all magic ingredient.

Risk a bit more giving. Next time you are wondering, "how much should I put in the box?" . . . triple what you decide.

Expect the best from life, and life will do it's best to give you exactly what you have asked of it!

There is no benefit in keeping this new formula for success to yourself. You won't steal a *better* lead on a rival by not telling him about your new found knowledge. If you are looking at life in the long term, then I am telling you that the only way forward is to

spread the word!

stage seven

spread the word

> Now this is not the end. It is not even the beginning of the end. But it is perhaps the end of the beginning...   *Winston Churchill*

We can't talk about success and being a good person, without touching on the subject of whatever it is you want to call it...Infinite Intelligence, the Supreme Being, Lord, Native State, the Wise One, Allah, the Divine Being, the Almighty or just plain old fashioned God?

Whatever you believe in is good, as long is it does other people good. If *your belief is good for others*, **then I think you will find that ultimately it has to be good for you**. Other peoples' viewpoints can be exciting and exhilarating, but usually only if they are different from your own. A wise person listens and takes note. Viewpoints on religion exist only because they have, or at one time did have, truth and relevance to life.

What is good for you, can be good for others... but not necessarily. Don't force your point of view down someone else's throat without invitation, and remember as I do now, that religion can be a very tricky subject to deal with.

I believe that *anything good is spiritual* in it's essence, and *anything bad is the opposite*...with *shades in between*.

Man is basically good, and it is that quality to which you should play at all times.

If you appeal to that side of a person's nature . . . with persistence . . . it will always be advantageous.

My viewpoint on God was a personal secret for a long time. When you talk about God you run the risk of alienating certain people who ordinarily you would like on your side. But my views are so simple and inoffensive, that I now see no reason why they cannot be shared.

I believe that you are God!

I believe that I am God. I believe that a stronger God appears when you and I get together. I believe that the ultimate God is the reunification of every Being back into one unit.

I believe that we were as one a long time ago. I think that we started this Universe as a game. The game got out of hand. We wanted something to do and we got it. We wanted a problem and we have it. We blame others, and the ultimate irony is when we blame God without seeing ourselves as part of that equation. How many times has God's will been blamed for failure?

We all come from the same place, and until you see your enemy as your potential ally, you decrease your chances of success.

I feel that we are an important part of this Universe.

It thrills me when I stop what I am doing and get the feeling of this universe flowing through me. If you take the viewpoint, even for just one minute, that the Universe is the whole, and we are the cells that comprise it, then you may feel a surge of *beautiful energy* surround you.

You have a body that is made up from millions of individual cells. When a cell gets sick, or begins to behave outside it's brief, the whole body can get ill. The cells can become malignant spreading growths... this would make them cancerous. They may have to be surgically removed, or they may kill the body that houses them before removal is possible.

We understand this process more and more each day. If we liken ourselves to a single body cell, like we can the whole body to the Universe, then we can see that deviant behaviour can have tragic consequences. We are all totally interdependent, just like the cells of a human body.

A toe cell may never come into contact with a nose cell, but they still need each other.

Likewise with a fellow Human Being in a country that you have no understanding of, and no desire to learn about...an interdependence still exists.

The brain cannot exist without a heart to pump

around the blood. The liver and kidneys are useless without a stomach...and all of these organs are made up of single cells...a similar relationship to the one we all have with the Universe.

We can fight other Planets and destroy the Universe that we all belong to. We may fight other Countries and destroy a section of the Planet with Nuclear Fallout. We can decide to fight our Fellow Countrymen because they live in a different part of the Country to us...they speak with a different accent and traditionally follow a different religion, even though they *worship the same God*.

We can fight street to street, and constantly remind ourselves of all the reasons why we should hate others. We can fight within our own families, and decide we no longer love the person we pledged ourselves to for the rest of our lives...

We can fight ourselves...or make peace.

We *are part of the same unit* and I am thrilled to know this. The more people that we can get agreeing to this principle, the easier and more joyful the World will become.

We have to rid ourselves of bigoted symbolism and intolerant tradition.

We cannot commit crimes in the name of tradition. We can't go to war saying that God is on our

143

side and not the other. It is just the same as the cancerous cells that eventually kill the host, and the tape worm that destroys the environment in which it lives.

We are all microcosms.

Similar patterns repeat themselves from the Universe as a whole, down to the single cell. If you embrace this theory you will only know *love and joy*.

Hatred and sorrow cannot exist in the presence of the BIG PICTURE!

If you allow yourself the privilege of this *BIG PICTURE*, then I guarantee you true success. Always see the whole picture. Ultimately that picture will be the Universe, and can be as trivial as being upset in your job because you got something wrong, but seeing that your upset is inconsequential, as the correction that was made, put the firm *you work for* in a healthier position. *THE FIRM IS THE UNIVERSE*.

You may be against the political party who currently govern your Country, but you must acknowledge them when they do something that benefits your Country. *THE COUNTRY IS THE UNIVERSE*.

You are against giving Aid to the Third World, because you think they should fend for themselves, then you learn that a British Doctor has just saved the life of a know nothing nobody from nowhere. Feel joy. *BOTH COUNTRIES ARE THE UNIVERSE*.

THE UNITED CELLS OF YOUR BODY ... THE UNITED MEMBERS OF YOUR FAMILY ... THE UNITED GROUPS OF YOUR TOWN ... THE UNITED TOWNS OF YOUR COUNTRY ... THE UNITED STATES OF EARTH ... THE UNITED PLANETS OF THE UNIVERSE.

Now is the time to get it together for the future. Let's get it right. We have the technology for physical abundance, and the technology of Human Science is understood more and more each day. We know how to programme the Sub Conscious Mind to make it serve us. We know how to encourage ourselves into a positive and happy frame of mind... *every single step you take... no matter how small or seemingly insignificant, has to have as it's basic motivation the desire to do some good.*

You have read this far, and there is now no turning back. You cannot have the knowledge I have given to you without putting it to work for the good of mankind. As you serve your fellow man, then you will be rewarded with an abundance of whatever is your fancy. I have told you how to programme your SM and make it work for you. *This data was a secret of the Universe.* You have to grant it this position of altitude and pledge your allegiance to the PAC.

The basic qualification for entry to the PAC... you must believe that anything can be achieved from a Positive Frame of Mind.

You are an Advanced PAC Practitioner and I take for granted the fact that you possess this basic requirement. The responsibility for the future of the Universe now *rests in your hands* and it is your job to show that we can all succeed with some basic guidance and a positive attitude. You have to teach by example. Your actions will be a direct reflection of your state of mind. You can demonstrate your intentions in very small ways to begin with. The size of your action is virtually immaterial.

One of the most thrilling experiences of my life, was when I consciously chose someone whom I had not liked for some time . . . and he had certainly not liked me for a similar length of time, and decided to contact him and be friends. It was a simple act, but when I saw it work, it was a powerful lesson. There was no need for this contact . . . no ulterior motive . . . I just wanted to do it. Can you imagine if everyone did this even once in their lives? Can you see how much Universal Negativity this would rid us of.

You can do it. You can decide right now to make your peace with the world. To banish any anger from your life, and demand the good things that are on offer. If you believe in mankind . . . and you may as well . . . it's here and most definitely tangible, then why not do this right now.

Demand the positive and banish the negative.

If you ultimately believe that you are related to

the rest of mankind, it makes giving to others so much easier. You are almost giving to yourself. Learn something new every day, and be willing to pass this data on for others to enjoy.

Keep positive mental image pictures in your mind, for it is the content of your mind that will transfer itself into physical reality.

Have you ever thought about someone whilst in a good mood, and remembered a time when you thought bad things about them? You feel a little embarrassed don't you? If you keep your thoughts positive, you can't feel bad about anyone. Always look at people from a good mood perspective. When you feel bad about someone, it's you who is feeling bad. *Why punish yourself.*

This is the game we are playing. The game of life in the physical universe. Decide to live in harmony with the world, and get what you want from life by serving others. Get more from life by working out how you can serve your fellow man even more. Is your cup half full or half empty? See the best in the worst and the worst never.

Your personal success starts with you...here and now!

This success will be as great as you can have great thoughts. It will come as quick as you can get into action. It will be as thorough as your plans are detailed. You will be as worthy as your outlook on others. You will be as interesting, as you are interested in others. Always listen more than you talk.

You are an Advanced PAC *Practitioner*!

GO AND SUCCEED!

Do you want to join the PAC?

PAC is an abbreviation for the Positive Attitude Club.

If, like me, you believe that absolutely anything can be achieved from a positive frame of mind, then I invite you to join the club.

There is no other qualification whatsoever!

I want people from all walks of life and educational backgrounds who embrace this philosophy to join forces.

Together, we can blaze a trail, and plan a healthy and prosperous future. We can help anyone or any situation, with our attitude.

Through the PAC, we can share our knowledge of the positive.

There are books and programmes available, that can form the basis of any positive plans you may have for your future.

As well as existing programmes, there is new material being written every day to help those who help themselves. I promise that the PAC will keep abreast of all data concerning the philosophy of positive attitude, and make it available to members.

The PAC will become the action station for the furtherance of positive attitudes throughout the world.

Read the PAC Mission Statement, and if you like what you see, and feel that you can win from subscribing to this idea . . .

Join the PAC . . . do it now . . . today!

I look forward to sharing a wonderful future with you!

Yours sincerely,

PHIL MURRAY
Leader of the PAC

THE PAC MISSION STATEMENT

ULTIMATE GOAL
Positive attitudes for all

THE PAC PHILOSOPHY
The improvement of personal life through positive attitudes, benefits mankind as a whole

GOALS

1 A large and increasing membership
2 We aid members' awareness of positive reading, writing and viewing materials
3 We help the world, with a constant output of positive affirmations from all members
4 We influence the world for the better in every way, shape and form
5 We show by example, that the PAC philosophy works
6 We influence the Media, and World Governments, with our philosophy
7 We have our headquarters and first clubhouse, in Mayfair, London
8 We are revered as an organisation of high principle, honour and integrity
9 We are consulted on any disagreements between peoples of the world, with the aim of solving all problems on a win for all basis
10 Happiness in the pursuit of our goals

PHIL MURRAY
Leader of the PAC

The PAC
**Purbeck, Mill Lane,
Felbridge, Surrey RH19 2PE**

Enrolment Form

**The Positive Attitude Club accepts
applications from anyone wishing to join.
All I ask is that you embrace the philosophy
contained in the Mission Statement.**

Name ....

Address ....

....

....

Telephone ....

Occupation ....

Enrolment Fee ....

The PAC is a brand new idea. The Organisation is as new as
the idea that spawned it. I have decided that for every copy
of the audio and book programme entitled *You Can
Always Get What You Want* that I sell, I shall invest 10
pence in the PAC. I suggest that you send the PAC, at the
address above, a minimum of £5 to enrol, or more if you
feel good about it. This is a positive statement of intent
from yourself, and it will also help towards the cost of
setting up the Club.

We intend to issue a monthly magazine, and until that is possible, I shall send you confirmation of membership, along with your membership number. The first 100 members will be called Founders. The following 400 members will be known as Founder Members. I appoint myself Leader of the PAC, and we shall elect a Cabinet as soon as possible. Each member will have one vote. Our first task will be to set an annual membership fee. If you wish to leave the PAC for whatever reason, then you shall be entitled to a full and unconditional refund of your initial enrolment fee.

I look forward to meeting you soon.

PHIL MURRAY
Leader of the PAC

BIBLIOGRAPHY

Napoleon Hill   *Success Through a Positive Mental Attitude*

Napoleon Hill   *Think and Grow Rich*

Napoleon Hill and W Clement Stone   *Success through a Positive Mental Attitude*

Napoleon Hill   *The Science of Personal Achievement* [Audio Programme]

Dale Carnegie   *How to Win Friends and Influence People*

Maxwell Maltz   *Psycho-Cybernetics*

Anthony Robbins   *Unlimited Power*

Anthony Robbins   *Awaken the Giant Within*

Brian Tracy   *Maximum Achievement*

Brian Tracy   *The Psychology of Achievement* [Audio Programme]

Stephen R Covey   *The 7 Habits of Highly Effective People*

Stephen R Covey   *Principle Centered Leadership Audio Cassette*

Colin Rose   *Accelerated Learning*

Dr Wayne W Dyer   *You'll see it when you believe it*

George S Clason   *The Richest Man In Babylon*

Dennis Waitley   *Seeds of Greatness*

Shad Helmstetter   *What To Say When You Talk To Yourself*

Harvey Mackay   *Swim With the Sharks Without Being Eaten Alive*

NLP Comprehensive   *NLP The New Technology Of Achievement* [Audio Programme]

Phil Murray Audio Products

Available from PeRFECT WORDS and MUSIC
Purbeck, Mill Lane, Felbridge, Surrey RH19 2PE.
Telephone 0342 322833

PWM 001 Vinyl 7 inch   *Another Geordie Christmas*
A light hearted look at Christmas in the North East of England

PWM 002 CD and Cassette album   *Plus*
11 melodic and original AOR songs, some written with
Dave Black

PWM 003 CD single   *Talk Talk*
The CD single not available on an album, which includes
two songs from *Plus*

PWM 004 CD and Cassette album   *Separate Holiday*
10 beautifully played and sung AOR songs, full of emotion
and excitement, all written by Phil

PWM 005 Cassette   *You Can Always Get*
                                What You Want
The abridged audio version of this book, delivered by Phil
in an exciting and motivational style

PWM 006 CD and Cassette   *Forever Again*
A stunning album of 12 brand new songs written by Phil . . .
a must for any collection

Phil Murray Fiction

Available from PeRFECT WORDS and MUSIC
Purbeck, Mill Lane, Felbridge, Surrey RH19 2PE.
Telephone 0342 322833

PWM 008 Book   *Through the Wall*
An exciting full length novel about a family's escape from
East Berlin. This story of the Beckanbauers, begins in 1945
and ends in 1961. Tense and harsh in places, this is a realistic
drama which focuses on the sheer determination of a family
to survive a cruel regime behind the old Iron Curtain.

The Phil Murray Success Programme...
is available LIVE

Goals and management styles...
Principles...
Getting things done...
Motivation and Inspiration...
Self Esteem...
Programming for CASH!
Sales and how to take control...
Visualisation...

Tailor made to suit *your* Company, we can bring the Seminar to you, or organise for you to attend one of our pre-arranged Seminars in your area.

Phil Murray is also available for PERSONAL POSITIVE ATTITUDE training, invaluable for personal and business life, professional sports, and general GOAL orientation.

Write or call PeRFECT WORDS and MUSIC for further details:

PeRFECT WORDS and MUSIC
Purbeck, Mill Lane,
Felbridge, Surrey RH19 2PE
Telephone: 0342 322833